Table of Contents

BEFORE YOU READ

WHAT KIND OF MEETINGS THIS BOOK ADDRESSES

This book focuses on conferences and meetings that are larger, longer and more geographically spread than the classic, everyday office meeting. They can include, for example, a two-day corporate meeting in a hotel with 45 participants, or a three-day, 950-participant association meeting taking place at a conference centre. We look at meetings and conferences such as the annual, international sales meeting, the annual user group meeting, the annual global meeting of the international association of the newspaper printing industry, etc.

We do not consider the small daily internal meetings in the office, where five people or even 10 meet in-house. We would refer to this as an office meeting.

☑ Yes this is the kind of meeting I'm interested in

WHICH ELEMENT OF MEETINGS WE TALK ABOUT

This book focuses on the content side of meetings - what happens during the meeting that is important to meeting owners - the meeting initiators, and their objectives. What changes in the minds of the participants, what influences the participants, what supports the objectives of the meeting in terms of learning, networking and motivation.

This book does not focus on the hospitality side of meetings nor do we talk about the travel side: we do not focus on flights, destinations, venues, accommodation or catering, etc.

☑ Yes this is of interest to me

TAKEAWAYS

This book talks about a vision for a new profession. It analyses the meeting industry from a semi-outside perspective and comes up with big-picture ideas and long-term options for the future. It is a roadmap for a new (Master's) degree or certificates leading to a new career path. It promotes the inclusion of new professionals, new knowledge and new faculties. It provides some concepts and ideas as food for thought, a basis for discussion and publication eventually leading to ongoing innovation for the industry's future.

☑ Yes this is of interest to me

MANIFESTO

This book is a manifesto. It is neither a manual nor a textbook. A manual for the profession of Meeting Architecture would probably be seven volumes, each of 600 pages. This book introduces broad elements of Meeting Architecture and merely provides a few examples of the hundreds of practical elements of Meeting Architecture. The book is a strategic thinking exercise, not a tactical, operational or practical handbook.

☑ Yes this is of interest to me

If you have checked all of the above boxes, this book will be of interest to you. You are probably a senior meeting professional or someone with an interest in the content side of meetings, an academic or a leader in the industry, a procurement or corporate C-level person, or maybe a student looking for future options.

1. Introduction

I began writing this book on Friday June 1, 2007, right after we moved to a house in the country. Each Friday I took the day off to write in the peace and quiet alongside a 240 hectare (2,400,000 sqm) nature reserve. Compared with North American national parks (some larger than my country) that is small, but for us it is huge.

As an entrepreneur I had to leave my team alone on these Fridays but did not worry one iota about work. This was possible only because of the great individuals who make up that team and I would like to thank each of them for making it so. Writing this book means a lot to me and being able to focus on it for one full day a week was just what I needed.

The house was built in the 70s and is a one-storey, neo-modern home with painted white brick walls and floor to ceiling windows. “Clearly inspired by Frank Lloyd Wright,” said Elling Hamso, a friend from Norway when he visited. He showed Facebook pictures of his parents’ house, which had also clearly been inspired by the same architect. It was the stillness and beauty of the location combined with the authentic modern architecture and the perfect quality of the house which made my wife Kristin and I decide to come to live here.

To a certain extent, this book is about that same combination of location and architecture. If I remember correctly, an ad in a meeting industry magazine a few year ago shouted “location, location, location” as the three key elements in successful meetings. A Google search for meeting and “location, location, location” results in 331,000 hits. This, in a way, reflects the state of the industry today. I myself am glad to have found my dream location, but without the house, built by a good architect, we could not live there with our two boys. Locations for meetings (destination and venue) are well developed in this industry, but can anyone tell me where I can find an architect to build the meeting?

Some people will say “I am a Meeting Architect” but in this book I demonstrate that no-one really can be, yet. This book is about the creation of Meeting Architecture, ultimately a Master’s degree in the subject, and its potential influence on meetings and the meetings industry. I ask questions about the state of the industry and the book challenges the current situation in several ways. It also addresses a number of topics in brief: each of these needs to be fleshed out with a book. This book is therefore not complete. It's the prologue of a series and, like the bibliography of this work, is merely exemplary.

The book may leave the reader with more questions than answers, and these questions need to be addressed in the near future; I do not have ready answers for all of them. It is also possible that this book may generate some adverse reaction or slight irritation, but if this causes people to discuss the topic it may well be a good thing. My hope is to gain the attention and engagement of a few people and the belief and support of many in order to make the meetings industry move forward in a direction that is currently covered by a kind of fog.

Although I am not a typical constituent of the meetings industry, let me assure you that for many years I have loved the industry and I know it has great growth potential. I, like so many, make a living from real face-to-face meetings: let no-one challenge the value of meetings or conferences when I'm around! Meetings are extremely valuable for individuals, organizations, society and the economy, but the industry does not play that tune as well as it could. The way the meetings industry does not use the real value of meetings is precisely the reason I had to write this book. The real value of meetings and conferences is seriously under-estimated, under-researched and under-documented and the future profession of Meeting Architecture will address that challenge more than ever before in a professional and scientific way. The industry is in good shape so it is probably not waiting for my ideas, but I believe addressing Meeting Architecture is a great opportunity to lift the industry to a higher, more strategic level. Getting that seat at the table will succeed only with the industry's support.

I wish the meeting industry a stable and strong future.

Maarten Vanneste, CMM

2. About the Author

Maarten Vanneste was born in 1963 as the third child in a family of five. His father was a music teacher and piano tuner, and his mother a housewife. One of many hobbies Maarten had as a child was photography, a hobby that stuck longer than many others. As a 14-year-old he installed equipment in his room and began to develop his own black and white pictures. Maarten's school results were average, but from the point of view of extra-curricular activities he was anything but average. President of the school council and organising open days at school as well as parties, he demonstrated his leadership skills.

The age of 18 is also a time to make a big decision: what next? Which profession to choose? Which degree from which university, or which diploma from which polytech? Maarten, with his wide range of interests, checked out some options, psychology among them. The degree seemed do-able but did not promise to be exciting enough. Too much theory and too many books, not enough practical hands-on... With his interest in photography, the next option was film director. Maarten went to Brussels and Ghent to check out the four polytechs where this was taught. One was too artistically oriented and another was too focused on national TV – all four seemed behind on technology. The new thing was video and film as in 16mm and 35mm – an old has-been medium he decided. As nothing really crystallised, a year-long world tour seemed a good option for taking the time to make up his mind.

In the summer of 1981 TV was on the news and one hot topic was the popularity of the home video recorder. VHS from Panasonic, Beta-max from Sony and Video-2000 from Philips – each of these cost about €2,000 but they were becoming very popular. Every family wanted one for playing rented movies and recording programmes on TV. Maarten's father saw the potential of this boom and suggested it would be great to produce educational videos for schools. He reasoned that his son's interest in film and psychology, combined with the state of education and Maarten's leadership skills could lead to only one conclusion: Maarten should start his own video production company. Mother agreed and so the career of a young man was put on course.

Interesting detail: Maarten's father is blind. Today, at 75-plus, he works with a normal PC and keyboard, writing, e-mailing and surfing the web.

3. How it all started

This chapter takes us briefly through the first 25 years, offering an understanding of why and how this project came to be.

April 1, 1982, and the company began as Abbit Video. When this book was written, that was 25 years ago. A great deal has happened in those 25 years – turns have been made and some tough nuts have been cracked. I feel that the past 25 years have taken me to a point where I'm ready for the next 25. All I have done, even before I started my company, seems to have come together. All the pieces of the puzzle are falling into place and this book, my first, is the medium to set it all down, clarify it and communicate it. It is also the stepping stone into the second half of my professional life.

More than anything else, this book aims at launching a project: the creation of a brand new profession – Meeting Architecture. In that sense it may also be a stepping stone to a new career phase for both many …

Video killed the radio star

When you are 18 and straight out of school, you don't really know anything about running a business, let alone setting one up.

I did, however, manage to produce a binder with some 50 pages of handwritten plans and calculations: today I would call that a business plan. A loan of 500,000 Belgian francs (some €15,000 or $22,500 in 2007) seemed a lot of money to me, but in retrospect I know it was not – certainly not enough to start a business, especially a video production company, in days when a video cassette cost as much as a video recorder does today.

I rented a house just around the corner from the street where I was born, came up with a company name and designed the logo so I could put it on the wall. Abbit was a name I dreamed up and was based on three criteria: alphabetically at the top of lists, the same number of letters as in video, and able to be pronounced internationally.

Than came the more difficult part: What equipment would need to be bought?

To cut a long story short: The one-tube camera and VHS editing system was not yet ready and I had invested 80% of my seeding finance, basically throwing away almost all of my start-up capital. Welcome to the real world…

As an 18-year-old, you also have no idea about sales and marketing. I put up my sign, opened my door, sat down by the phone and started waiting. How about that for a marketing campaign!

Everyone can imagine what happened next. Not a lot.
But this boy wasn't going to sit still for long.

Jolly July

Hildegart and myself in the editing studio

One of the things I did before opening the company in the summer of '82 was to start a new non-profit project named Jolly July. Together with friends and with support from our local CC (cultural centre) we organised weekly public creative activities and events in the open air, in what were otherwise dead quiet summers. This resulted in several other things: one of those friends, Hildegart, later became our first employee, and Abbit Video was able to survive its critical first three years by undertaking similar activities.

One of these results involved a local punk band which sold me its sound system as its members went their own ways. An old mixing table with a few cheap microphones, a 100-watt amplifier and two enormous loudspeakers made up the gear. I rented these out for parties and, with my video background and a few second-hand TV sets, I began organising video parties, which were very innovative events in those days. I travelled all the way to the Virgin Megastore in London just to buy the latest VHS tapes with popular video clips. In the summer of 1983 we visited about 10 clubs on a tour of the Belgian coast sponsored by Safari, a new beverage. The Safari importer paid us €12,500 as our sole sponsor; the same amount I had had as starting capital just one year earlier. This is probably the right place to thank the person who trusted us back then.

Tour de France

Another highlight of the early years came in 1988, our sixth year, and this was the Tour de France. A Brussels-based company had won a contract to set up a large open-air dance club in the cities and villages where the Tour de France arrived. Abbit Video was contracted for the video part of the deal, a contract of some €50,000 in today's value. This one contract was as large as the turnover of our entire first year.

The dance club lasted for just the one year because most cyclists go to bed early during the Tour and loud music until midnight is simply not compatible with a good night's sleep.

From AV to business focus

In the years that these events were taking place, Abbit Video was also growing into increasing amounts of corporate work. Video productions, AV support for trade shows, opening events and meetings became increasingly evident in the diary. Most of the events we did were, to an extent, a lot like meetings and conferences. A large group of people, presentations, some sound, light, projection, etc. One clear stepping stone into meetings for Abbit came with a call from a national sales manager in the late 80s. He was organising his national sales meetings for a pharmaceutical company and invited me for a talk about equipment. We combined sound, light, projection, presentation, video production and photography – the first real 'meeting support' moment had arrived.

The club and party scene had one big disadvantage: it paid late and sometimes not at all, and always involved working at night. Corporate clients were clearly better clients and the added value we could provide in meetings was much more of an intellectual challenge. We said goodbye to the night scene around 1987, a break which would lead to many similar decisions in the years to come. The next step was the closing of our doors, meaning that we stopped renting out items such as TVs and video cameras to individual consumers – our decision to go for professional work and corporate clients was firm.
The next major step was to stop selling equipment in 1992. Selling is a very different business and requires a different business model as a whole. If we really wished to focus on meetings we had to organise ourselves completely towards meeting the specific needs and requirements of meetings. Our vision and our approach to the market became more and more focused.

One of the last major decisions in that evolution was the end of dry hire. This meant a local venue or company could no longer knock on our door to rent a flipchart and a microphone, or a TV and a video. We made the radical decision to go for projects, specifically meetings and conferences.

Abbit was no longer a typical AV company because it offered a wide range of integrated services to a narrow market. Neither was it a production company. It had in-house equipment in contrast with most production companies which select the type of equipment they need for the kind of event they're producing. We were focusing on meetings and we used specialised equipment and our own control over that equipment to guarantee quality.

The Dirk Reyn meetings

One of the most inspiring clients I have worked with is Dirk Reyn of a pharmaceutical company based in a village five minutes from Turnhout. It is Belgium's largest such company and operates on a global scale. Dirk Reyn was international product manager for a product with an active component for treating a variety of stomach complaints. It was a potential success story in 1990 when he invited us to his office based on what he heard from a colleague, who had worked with Abbit for national sales meetings.

From day one Dirk challenged us to come up with new and innovative ideas to make his meetings more successful. Like no one I had met previously, he understood the potential of meetings. He saw the potential in education, networking and motivation. Working with around 100 national product and marketing managers, he looked to create an experience that would stick. In order to do so he stimulated us to open up all our registers, dig deep into our potential and to think out of the box. This is exactly what made us perform at our best with all the available creative, technical and early technological tools. For eight years in a row, from 1991 to 1998, we put as much innovation as possible into every meeting. The concept of meeting support, or Meeting Architecture (see later in this book) did not exist at this time, but Dirk in fact spent, like a true Meeting Architect, lots of time and resources in analysing, designing and executing the meetings on the content side. For the travel and hospitality side he worked with a travel agency from the UK, and for the content side with a medical communications agency from the UK and Abbit. The travel, the hotel, the receptions and dinners were all taken care of by the travel agency, so we could focus fully on the meeting itself and creating that educational, networking and motivational experience for the participants, inside the meeting

First we got the basics right – good sound, good light, a professional stage and set, and good quality presentations. This was all operated by a team of five to six qualified and specialised technicians. Dirk was the first to ask us if we could also do PowerPoint presentations besides 35mm slides. I went straight to the computer shop and bought our first ever PowerPoint, version 2.0.

Besides taking good care of those basics, we did lots of creative and innovative things. Long before the digital camera existed, we produced on-site personalised certificates of attendance with the pictures of the participants included. In those days we took photos with a 35mm reflex camera and took the film to a developer in town. The pictures were printed and rushed back to the hotel, before printing the result on sophisticated paper and having each certificate signed by the meeting organisers. At the end of the closing session every participant was excited to receive them. Most people displayed them on their office wall for at least a year.

Another idea we executed for Dirk was the welcome tapes at Barcelona. A sound cassette with a welcome word from Dirk and the meeting's theme music was played to participants on their taxi trip from the airport to their hotel. It was a simple and low-cost tool, but what an impact it had. Not only were the participants surprised to get a message half-way through their journey, but they also arrived prepared and excited, having heard the meeting host introduce the key issues of that meeting. It was an exciting (motivational) and informative (educational) experience.

Video on wheels

not exactly portable but in the 90's that's what it took. Today one laptop is all it takes.

Once on-site video editing became an option, we started making closing videos. Interviews with participants were part of this from the start. Soon we were making a daily news bulletin about the previous day, a great way to wake up and start the new day. Another application of on-site editing was for every country representative to make a 30-second promotional video which would "sell" that country's marketing materials to other countries. This co-creation and educating of each other was exceptional in days when the average speaker with slides gave the audience a three-minute Q&A and that was it for interactivity.

The Product Promotion Club was another great way of involving and motivating the audience, stimulating peer to peer learning and driving the networking. The promotion club gave each country a small table and panel to display its promotional material. In a short time everyone present was able to discover great ideas from the other countries and meet the people from that country. All key objectives were taken care of by this activity:

Learning:	seeing good ideas from other countries and discussing them
Networking:	meeting peers form other countries
Motivation:	allowing professionals to show their creations, to share and be listened to.

It was one of the most valuable components of the meeting.

These and many more intense and creative ideas were all presented under a meeting logo which evolved only slightly each year and repeated the colours and basic shapes, turning it into a recognisable sequel. The main goal was set at a certain budget in sales by the year 2000 and, as the first meeting was held in Cyprus, the meetings were called Olympus 2000 after the Greek god and the mountain.

The key messages remained the same all those years and were called the Four Cs: Culture, Creativity, Consistency, Commitment. These four C words were always present and served as an umbrella for every topic addressed.

Serial Meetings

This brings us to a more strategic level. Dirk had organised these meetings as a series. There was an end goal and even an end date for this series. Each meeting reported on progress and kept clearly focused on the end goal. Each was a stepping stone to the next and incremental progress was made. That kind of real long-term vision in serial meetings is still rare today. Obviously, long term collaboration with suppliers and a buy-in from management were crucial.

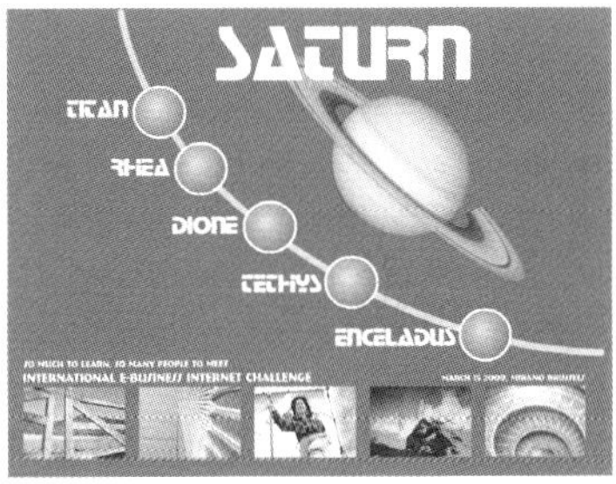

Dirk Reyn hit the target before the planned date and we are proud that we were part of a process where meetings really were the driving force and the glue that kept it all together. He accomplished a paradigm shift in my mind, although I only woke up to it a few years later. It was Dirk's focus, drive and creativity that planted the seed of the concept of Meeting Support, the Meeting Objective Matrix® and eventually Meeting Architecture. If anyone was ever a true meeting content architect, it was Dirk. Today it is still rare that a meeting owner is so much involved in such an holistic way with analysing, designing and executing the meeting.

Let's focus on meetings

In May 1998 Abbit organised its first own internal meeting named X-tra and themed *"Let's focus on Meetings"*. This was the year we officially decided to concentrate entirely on the meeting and conference market. We had great value to add, we liked the product and we felt there was a healthy market.

A while before that, I had decided to visit agencies in the Brussels area that were listed as conference organisers in the yellow pages. One of these was Nikitra and as I was waiting in their lobby I browsed through national magazines about meetings and events. I had had no idea there were magazines about meetings so I immediately subscribed and was soon invited by the magazine owner Eric De Ridder for a focus group meeting about the direction and future of the magazine. Since I was so convinced meetings were our company's future I went without hesitation. There I met the president of the Belgian Chapter of MPI. MPI stands for Meeting Professionals International, an association with at that time around 16,000 members and currently (2008) more than 23,000. I immediately signed up, became a member of the board and three years later became president of the Belgian Chapter. Today I am an internationally active member and a regular supporter and sponsor of the Belgian Chapter. MPI is the largest global association in a wonderful industry, a young industry. MPI has existed for some 40 years now and the industry has grown a lot in those years, becoming truly professional.

The MPI effect

From then on, things really started to move. In 1999 Abbit grew by 72% and in 2000 by more than 40%. I checked the details and this growth was completely thanks to MPI, through which I could network with meeting planners who became clients. Some are large organisations from both Europe and the US, and organise annual meetings in many European countries.

As a host sponsor of MPI's European conference for five years in a row, our company was really able to understand and connect with a group of meeting professionals and learned a lot in doing so.

In 2002 we were looking for a good way to describe our activities. By then we provided almost everything there was available to support meetings in their key objectives. We were not an average AV company, we were not a production company and we were not a PCO or an event agency. After an internal meeting, one of our team came up with the term "Meeting Support", which we adopted. We now call our company Abbit Meeting Support. We provide meeting support for our clients and we have meeting support managers and meeting support technicians.

MPI also provided me with the opportunity to talk to a lot of professionals and also to speak to audiences of up to 2,000 people. This made me think, discuss and prepare presentations, and to write down and rethink my ideas about this industry – a great sounding board for ideas and concepts that helped me stay focused and really develop our company's strategy and the content of this book.

The CMM course (Certification in Meeting Management) was another MPI breakthrough moment where I was pushed into thinking and organising my professional life in a strategic way. It also made me write the business plan for what today is the Meeting Support Institute (see p. 98). In addition to my many friends amongst MPI's global membership, I would like particularly to thank Didier Scaillet, a long-time MPI staff member, for all his support and guidance.

In 25 years we have evolved a great deal. Over the past few years I have kept working on and thinking about what it is we do and where our true value lies. This did not stop at meeting support and I think the pinnacle is now in sight. The next big thing on the horizon is Meeting Architecture and I look forward to being part of making that happen in the coming 25 years. The following chapters will address the path of this step by step.

The path towards the writing of this book began with an 18-year-old starting his own video production company in 1982. Five years of surviving, 10 years of focusing and 10 years of innovation is what made me realise that the time was right for taking the next step. Seeing this industry evolve from the shell for meetings to both the shell and the substance of meetings is a dream. I will be proud if I can play a small part in that dream.

NEXT CHAPTERS

In the next chapters I will share my view on the meetings industry from the outside in, then talk about what I observe to be clearly missing, and how we could develop and support the under-developed 'content' side of meetings. In the final three chapters I deal with how Meeting Architecture as a profession could be the catalyst to make it all happen.

4. The meeting industry

What do we have

In 1998 I started to go to our industry's trade shows. This was a real eye-opener.
What I saw was only meeting venues (conference centres, hotels and hotel chains) and meeting destinations (countries, regions and cities). I thought I was part of the meetings industry but I saw nothing that related to my world in this gigantic global Meeting Industry trade show in Geneva. No educators, no AV companies, no production companies, no presentation specialists, meeting photographers... There was nothing about education, networking or motivation. I felt strangely awkward in the middle of the biggest event of the industry I had become a part of. I felt like the little boy in 'The Emperor's New Clothes' and wanted to shout "the emperor is naked!". I did not understand how this could be called the meeting industry by a whole community although there clearly was no direct connection to a meeting's core objectives. This was only about the environment in which meetings could take place, the shell, and I was looking for the substance.

This was my big wake-up call. The industry of meeting professionals had clearly shifted in one direction – that of hospitality and business tourism. Or did just a part of the tourism industry adopt the name "meeting industry" in order to be taken more seriously?

However it came to be, this industry did not feel like mine and so a quest started. Where did I belong? Where did my company belong? I started a long journey, looking for a place where I would feel professionally at home, a place with peers – people with an interest in the core of meetings, the content side of meetings. I did not find it.
Today I have found the words to describe what I only instinctively felt in the late 1990s. The fact that I came to a good understanding of the industry, with the big question lingering in the back of my mind, made me see things and come to some critical conclusions. This is the story I want to share with one goal: to help the meeting industry move to its next level, to grow and prosper.

> "The 2008 meeting industry is proficient in creating the shell in which meetings take place. The only thing we have to do is look inside that shell, put in a grain of sand and, after a few years, harvest the pearl."

Magazines

Getting more and more into the meetings industry, I got more and more magazines. Today I am aware of some 30 different magazines of which I get about 10 on a monthly basis. These are magazines from Europe, North America and Asia.

In 2006 I made an analysis of a series of magazines. In order to see where the real emphasis of this industry lay, I thought it could be a good exercise to count and analyse the advertising. Advertising costs a lot of money so it shows where the money is and where the real players of the industry are. And guess what? Some 98.5% of all advertising was about destinations (countries, states, regions, cities) and venues (mostly hotel chains).

No explanation is needed to understand that the meeting industry currently exists only thanks to the hospitality industry. Looking at editorial content confirms that it's mainly about the hospitality side with some on personal and professional development – topics such as time management, leadership, risk management, entrepreneurial skills, work-life balance, stress management, conflict management and the like. These are not directly connected to the meeting industry but generally applicable to personal, work or business life.

Seldom will you find an article which addresses the substance of meetings – topics such as how to innovate presentations and how to raise levels of interactivity; what kind of educational methods can be applied at meetings and which to use when? What can be done and what should not be done in order to harvest the wisdom of all meeting participants? What methods or tools can a meeting planner use at a corporate meeting to increase cross-divisional collaboration? How can teams be created and task forces started at a meeting? And so on…

Multi-billion dollar industry

Is the meeting industry part of the business travel / tourism / hospitality industry?
I guess it is and for many reasons it seems very natural that the meetings industry is so strongly connected to the tourism / hospitality industry.

Looking at the globalisation of companies and associations alike, the number of international meetings and conferences has been growing a great deal in recent decades.

If we organise an international conference for sales managers of a multinational company, only one of them can perhaps travel by car: the one who lives in the host country. All other participants must fly in or come by train. If a global conference on diabetes organised by the IDF (the International Diabetes Foundation) takes place on a different continent every year, it enables professional participants of all continents to participate once in a while in the top educational event in their field. This IDF conference brings together some 15,000 who all have to fly in and stay a few nights in a hotel, and generates millions of dollars in aircraft seats and room nights. The airline industry gets 40% of its business from meetings. The hotel industry is 56% based on business travellers of whom 75% travel for a meeting or a conference.

And then one realises that a participant in a residential conference (stays in a hotel) spends on an average €250 a day in the city the conference takes place. The industry may not be aware, but its total turnover in travel, hotels, etc. was US$122.31 billion in 2004, making it the 29th largest industry in the US.

	Revenue	Meetings	Proportion
Airlines	131.5 billion	17.39 billion	13.2%
Hotel industry	113.7 billion	36.8 billion	32.4%

(CIC, 2005)

The companies operating here are large companies such as hotel chains and airlines – companies with thousands of employees, global brands and multi-million dollar marketing budgets in contrast to the companies working on the substance side of meetings. These are usually small or even one-man companies such as moderators, speaker trainers, presentation designers, meeting designers up to small or medium sized companies like meeting-focused AV and production companies, or sections of PCOs, parts of event agencies and sometimes a department in a marketing and communication agency.

In most cases there is only a partial focus on meetings. These are companies or people doing many things, and also meetings. Real meeting-focused companies are hard to find. Here too, it seems natural that this part of the meetings industry is nowhere to be seen. It is totally fragmented and too small even to have a marketing budget let alone a brand.

So yes, the meetings industry is currently part of the hospitality (travel and tourism) industry. That is my conclusion, as an observer, looking in from the outside. I see an opportunity and how fast that opportunity will develop is entirely up to the industry.

The little brother

The Economic Impact Study 2004 by the CIC (Convention Industry Council) shows a breakdown by expenditure in direct spending on conventions and exhibitions. In travel, hotel and F&B (Food and Beverage) we see about 85% of total spending. Some 15% goes to business services (12%), technology (0.2%) and other (3%). We must look for what is spent on the content side in the latter figure.

CIC defines Direct Spending as: *"All expenditures associated with an event that flow into the host destination's local economy. Direct spending includes attendee spending, exhibitor spending and event organizer spending."*
This means in fact that we do not have numbers on how much is spent on the content side of meetings.

The table on page 44 shows one corporate example in which 10% is spent on production and AV and 90% on logistics. Is this typical of how meetings are budgeted? Or are we missing information we need to provide a complete picture? I would have to conclude that the meeting industry's average spending on supporting actual meeting objectives is relatively small.

Degrees for this industry

Conference management studies or a degree in meeting management are in most cases a section of tourism departments. Professor Rob Davidson, whom I met at the annual conference of the Netherlands MPI chapter, is Senior Lecturer in Business Travel and Tourism at Westminster University in London and teaches a course in Meeting Management. He had read some of my articles and joined my session about the content side of meetings and how this is currently not developed or is under-developed. The session also touched briefly on the focus of current meeting management education and

what it could be or what should be added to make it complete.
After the presentation he came to me and explained enthusiastically how he now realised there was a gigantic opportunity for the meeting management courses and degrees and also for the meetings industry as a whole. He agreed that the current curriculum is mainly geared towards the tourism and hospitality side of the meetings industry and does not teach about the real reasons why people organise meetings: the objectives of meetings. The "what to achieve in the minds of participants" part is not addressed. Nothing is taught about how the Learning, Networking or Motivation among participants can be designed, supported, met or measured.

The geographical connection

Besides the big global players – the airlines and large hotel chains – there are also large local hospitality and tourism players. Every country, many regions and most cities have an office promoting themselves as a destination for incentives, conferences and meetings. These are called the CVBs, short for Convention Visitors Bureau. Most of the time these offices form part of the tourism departments for obvious reasons. The city sees conference participants as tourists because they generate income in the local tourism industry: besides venues and hotels a lot of other spending takes place in restaurants and shopping for example. The $128 billion for the US alone generates local taxes too.

The real reason why meetings are organised generates earnings elsewhere, not at the destination. What people learn at a conference in Denver may be applied, and therefore generate an income, in South Africa and dozens of other countries. So for Denver, the stakes are totally in the tourism and hospitality side of the meeting, not in the meeting objectives. These bureaus are governmentally and politically connected and supported for tax reasons. A city that has annually 100,000 one-day visits for conferences generates some €25,000,000 in turnover for hotels, restaurants, gift and souvenir shops, entertainment establishments and the like for that city. In turn this generates two to three million in taxes for the city and much more in labour taxes and other taxes[1] for the country. Part of that is used to fund the CVB.

1 *The CIC Economic Impact Study shows direct tax revenue of US$ 21.40 billion in the US.*

This explains why the meeting industry is part of the tourism industry. And because it is part of the tourism industry it cultivates its tourism side. This makes it less concerned about things that meetings are really about. Because it is less knowledgeable on the content side of meetings it remains part of the tourism industry and attracts hospitality professionals. Is this is the industry's Catch 22?

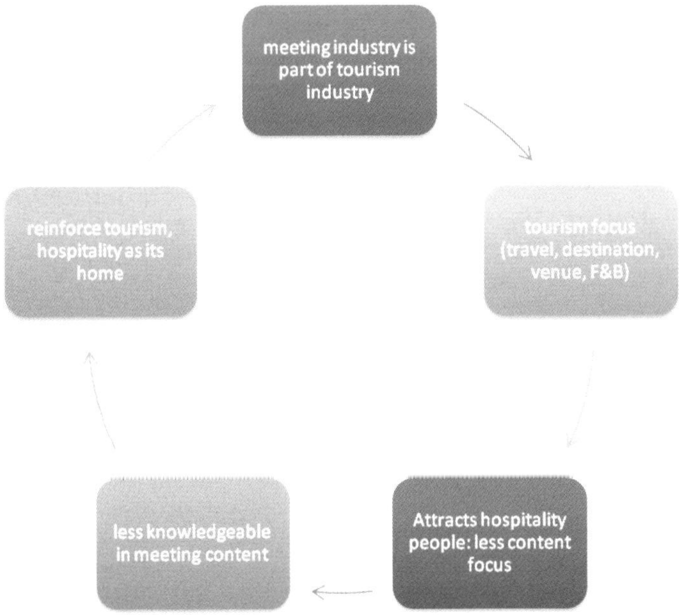

"The tourism Catch 22" that marries the meeting industry to the tourism industry

Example: Members of the Antwerp CVB

Province of Antwerp	Horeca section for hotels	De Lijn (public bus services)	University of Antwerp	Unizo (organisation for SMEs)
City of Antwerp	City Region Antwerp – venues	NMBS (Railway)	(GOM) Regional Development Agency for Antwerp	Voka – Chamber of Commerce
City of Mechelen	Green Region Kempen (venues)	SN Brussels Airlines	High Council for Diamonds	
Tourism dept of the Province of Antwerp	City Region of Mechelen (venues)	VLM Airlines	Provincial Museums	

This table shows the natural leading position of travel / tourism / hospitality entities in CVBs.

Complexity of meeting planning

Meeting planners are individuals with a degree in meeting management who visit the meetings trade shows and read the meetings magazines. They are the target audience of the hotel and destinations industry which endeavours to get groups into their own particular city or hotels.

Meeting planners have challenging jobs. On average they are extremely busy, travel a lot and work under the constant pressure of absolute and sometimes extreme deadlines on the one hand and budgetary constraints on the other.

Some 75% of meeting planners in the pharmaceutical industry say they have little or no impact on the content side of the meetings. They do, however, have a big say in the hospitality side of the meetings. Meeting planners search for an appropriate venue, book and contract meeting space and bedrooms, arrange travel, arrange buses for transfers, organise meals and coffee breaks, find and book special venues for the closing dinner, book restaurants for the free evening, etc. And all that for a diverse group with all kinds of special dietary and other individual needs. Then there are the invitations, registration, payments, badges, hostesses, welcome desks, etc.

On an international scale this job requires a great deal of knowledge about cultural differences in areas such as food, habits, time, etiquette, safety, shipping, customs, finance and the like.

Many meeting planners organise consecutive multiple meetings for their company, association or clients. They travel around the world to carry out site inspections and to assist at the meetings they organise. Travelling is what many meeting planners get so much of that a free trip to Lisbon does not excite them much.

Meeting planners have absolute deadlines, which means they can not postpone the opening reception by a day for whatever reason. The deadline for the construction of a new building is not absolute. If a building is ready one month late, we still have a building. If a meeting starts one day late, everything is lost. On top of this, the planners usually don't get sufficient lead time from the people they work for: the meeting owners. Finding and contracting a venue and planning all that needs to be in place is seriously under-estimated in many cases. This is why meeting planners are hard-working, task-switching, stress-resistant and well-organised professionals. Almost 75% of them are female as MPI membership numbers show. All of their time, attention and energy is needed to organise the travel and hospitality side of things for one meeting or conference after another. With a workload like this, it seems quite normal that many of these meeting professionals are not looking for extra work by getting involved in the content side of the meeting.

Most meeting planners are pleased that they can focus on hospitality. Some others would like to move into the content side and become more involved in the substance and driving the objectives of the meeting.

This latter category has the potential to become what this book is all about – Meeting Architects.

Most meeting planners have their minds and, perhaps more importantly, their hearts anchored in hospitality. This is what they love to do: getting people together and making sure everyone has a good time and feels well looked after – the true hospitality mindset which is fundamental to the meetings industry.

Cables and buttons

Most meeting planners are not overly educated in technical matters such as AV and ICT. Many planners are, however, asked to book AV for a meeting and do so because it is part of their job, not because they get excited about mixing tables, microphones, light dimmers, LCD screens, internet connections, voting systems, networking technology and the like.

not everyone likes buttons, and that is a good thing for meetings.

In these circumstances, it is challenging for a production or technology company to be faced with a client who does not really value the technical things but puts his or her heart and soul into the five-course dinner rather than the closing presentation. It is a tough collaboration with a product that is an intangible service and difficult to demonstrate, unlike a venue, a meeting room and even a dinner. Showing what the closing video will look like is simply not possible until it is time for the closing session.

In these circumstances it is quite normal and acceptable that the content, the objectives of the meeting, are left untouched by the meeting planner. The meeting owner, who is a marketing director or sales manager, is on his own for meeting content, in some cases supported by a marketing or communication person. Many core elements of meetings are not addressed at all: the need for designing the programme, selecting the right formats, training the speakers, involving facilitators, investigating and selecting the right networking tools, maximising the before and after potential of a meeting. Only a few meeting owners really spend time on these key issues and even fewer have the fully informed and specialised people to rely on.

Meeting owner is not a profession

The words "meeting owner" appear about 130 times in this book. Some organisations will call such a person a meeting sponsor or meeting host; there is no official name for the role. What it means is the person, or in some cases a small team, who owns the meeting in the sense that he or she decides a meeting or conference is needed, owns the budget and decides on what the objectives of the meeting are. The meeting owner is the initiator of the meeting and therefore decides on the life or death of a meeting. Although the industry trade shows rarely sees one, they are our ultimate clients. Although meeting owners don't read our magazines, and are rarely member of meeting industry associations they ultimately decide about our very existence.

the meeting owner decides on the life or death of a meeting.

The meeting owner can be many different things. In most cases he or she is a marketing manager but can also be an HR manager, a sales director, a CEO or hold a range of other positions. In none of these cases is being a meeting owner an actual profession. In most cases, meeting owners are temps and, at best, part-time for a few weeks. In other words, being a meeting owner is not a profession. You can not go to meeting owner courses, "The Meeting Owner" magazine does not exist and there is no association of meeting owners.

Who do meeting owners talk to when they start the next meeting project? The meeting planner does so and will take the hospitality side out of his or her hands and manage all the logistics needs of the participants. On the content side there is the marketing department which, in most cases, will not have a meeting specialist either. Marketing will be supporting the look and feel, design, branding, printed matters, etc. Most meeting owners are convinced they know the meeting's objectives and how to achieve them. They are convinced that they know all they need to know about driving the objectives and designing the meeting in a way that supports the goals.

They spend hundreds of thousands or even millions on a meeting based on their own experience as a temp. They take hundreds of professionals out of their work for days with only limited help in limited areas of the meeting from non-specialised people. They face the company's 500 top clients using their gut feeling rather than a professional methodology in the design. They use the same format as last year, based only on the participants' expressed satisfaction. This is really how it works in most meetings. In March 2008 this was confirmed to me by one of the world's largest oil companies, which has no standard procedures for organising the content side of meetings. They have procurement in place for the travel and hotel spend, but no SOP (Standard Operating Procedure) for the content side.

lots of people spending lots of time in lots of plans

When building a small warehouse for half a million dollars, every global company will work with a strict procedure, a carefully selected architect and a construction company and appointing a project manager and a construction site manager. When spending double or more on a meeting, none of that careful and good governance is to be seen.

I have yet to meet the meeting owner who has an SOP or even a methodology for managing the content side of meetings. Meeting owners are temps, not professionals, so who can blame them?

It is my experience that once meeting owners understand there is potential help to guide them through a process, they may set aside their pride and welcome assistance above and beyond the support they have experienced to date. Meeting owners will accept help if they see an organised, knowledgeable and systematic approach to building objective-based meetings.

meeting owners are temps

I have yet to encounter the first meeting owner who even has all of his or her meeting objectives written down in an orderly fashion. Most meeting owners verbally describe the meeting objective – singular, not plural. I know that meeting objectives are always manifold but remain undiscovered and unaddressed. A few hours spent in a structured brainstorm enables most meeting owners to discover many more objectives they have never considered. Meeting owners need help.

From who? That is the question. There is no-one out there with all the knowledge and skills let alone a standardised process that is applicable on a corporate-wide basis. When I speak about this topic, some participants such as senior planners and PCOs will say they can do this, but they also agree that they don't know all there is to know about how to do a professional job. I have been working on and studying this matter for a few years now and it is my belief that I have merely discovered 10% of what is out there. Tons of research needs to be carried out, just to locate and gather all of the relevant existing knowledge and tools that will have an impact. Then individuals need to study the material and only then can professionals emerge to help the meeting owner get a grip on the substance of his or her meeting.

4,900% difference

This is how we get to see some strange and extreme spending behaviour. Let's compare two cases I witnessed personally. One group was of 950 high-ranking military personnel while the other involved 120 product managers and marketing people from a pharmaceutical company. The meeting planner for the group of 950 spends €5 a person per day on all the AV, production, ICT costs etc.

The meeting owner of the group of spends €250 a person per day, including a big set, opening video, perfect AV, the best presentation technology, spectacular lighting, great speaker support, facilitation and similar. There's a massive 4,900% difference and still both meeting owners feel they are doing a good job.

The interesting observation in this case is that both groups use the same five-star hotel in London and spend €300 to €400 a person per day on the conference package, meals and a room night. Both parties understand the value of good hospitality for meetings, but they differ massively in their approach to the development and support of the meeting objectives.

Looking at the cost per person per day is not something that occurs on the meeting content side. The opening video costs €5,000 and it is not common practice to divide that by the 120 participants. The hospitality side is calculated, offered and budgeted per person as the cost for a flight, room nights and meals.

Budgetary Balance Between Body & Brain

If we call the meeting content side the brain side of meetings – learning, networking and motivation takes place mainly in the brain – and we call the hospitality side the body side – travelling, sleeping and meals are mainly body support functions – then one could analyse the resources allocated to Body and Brain at a meeting. For a particular meeting, or a particular company or association, a balance will be reached at a certain level that is appropriate for that meeting and that organisation.

This is what we call the Budgetary Balance Between Body and Brain..

BBBBB

Comparing different meetings, we will see that one meeting pays no attention to the brain side with a 90/10 ratio while another reaches an almost 50/50 balance. Can we call a meeting which spends 90% of its budget on hospitality a meeting? Or should we call it an incentive? What is your acceptable budgetary balance between body and brain? What is a good balance in order to maximise the meeting's potential?

It is not, of course, as black and white as I've presented it. Great hospitality also influences the learning, networking and especially the motivation.

It is clear that good hospitality is fundamental. We can not build a meeting without that foundation. It needs to be good or participants begin the day in a bad mood and everything else is a waste of time. On the other side, one should not forget to construct an equally great meeting on top of that great foundation. Both should be appropriately addressed and resources should be spent in a balanced way in order to get the best results leading to successful meetings.

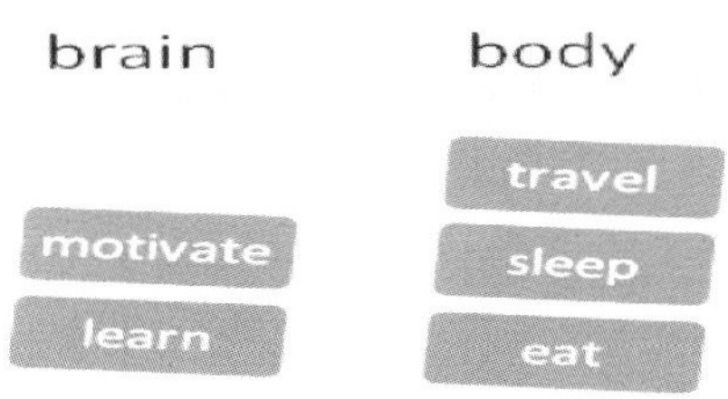

the balance between the two crucial sides of meetings must be addressed in order to achieve productive meetings

Best of both worlds

I consider a meeting or conference the most complete type of activity in the MICE industry. MICE stands for Meetings, Incentives, Conferences and Events. Many English-language people don't like the term because mice is the plural of mouse and they will be happy to see the current trend towards "Meeting Industry" as the generic term.

I believe a good meeting contains all of the MICE elements. The I (incentive) and the E (event) elements are all part of a good meeting – an incentive as in a motivational trip to stimulate people's performance. An incentive trip involves a nice destination, a great venue, fun activities, entertainment and great catering. In many cases it also includes travelling to exotic places and impressive hotel accommodation. These are purely travel and hospitality elements combined to forge a great experience. Any good conference puts a great deal of effort, with help from a meeting planner, into making all of those elements optimally support the participants' wellbeing. A good meeting is, in that sense, partially an incentive, and its motivational effect is one of the three key objectives in meetings besides education and networking.

An event is usual a non-residential stage-focused activity. A group, usually national so not involving much travel, gets together at a venue for a show, entertainment and some product presentation. The staging, production and creation of a special 'experience' are the main focal points for the event. Any good conference will also have those elements combined in an opening and/or closing session. A performance on stage, a spectacular opening show or video and a big production are some of the elements which overlap in events and great meetings. Motivation is again the most important key objective combined with some limited networking and learning.

As a real meeting and conference person, I tend to think that an incentive or an event are, in fact, meetings that lack a few things.
An incentive is a meeting that lacks education.
An event is a short meeting that invests highly in entertainment.
This does not mean that incentives or events should become meetings, but they all contain elements of meetings. Meetings and conferences also need to pay attention to their incentive and event side in order to be complete and better. On top of the incentive elements and the event elements, a meeting adds various unique features that make it a meeting. These elements are mainly educational and networking but also, in a very specific way, motivational. An opening video, an impressive set, a great keynote speech, organised networking, real interactivity and participation by those involved are all such motivational elements.

The budgetary balance should be taken into consideration when analysing whether a meeting is a meeting or an incentive. A meeting that spends 90% of its entire budget on the hospitality side may be considered an incentive rather than a meeting.

AV companies

On the content side of meetings, AV (audio-visual) material is the foundation. Good AV is a must for basic performance at meetings. Understanding the speaker and being able to read the slides is a must, so AV is a crucial component for any meeting. Many AV companies are at the first level of the value chain. They take the order and bring whatever a meeting planner asks.

The second level in the value chain is when an AV company asks questions such as "how many people do we expect in which room" in order to decide how many loudspeakers are needed. This is when an AV company adds some value.

The final level takes us into the key objectives of the meeting. Once these are analysed and understood, the AV company may advise on the use of a voting system or Audience Response System because it understands that gathering opinions or creating more active participation is an objective. An AV company may advise spending less on the opening show and more in the break-out rooms because education seems to be the key objective.

Very few AV companies do that because of different interests and a lack of focus on meetings and conferences. AV companies are like meeting owners: they are focused only part-time on meetings.

Most AV companies do everything for everyone as Abbit did in the 1980s. First they sell equipment and install it in meeting rooms, cafés, theatres, etc. Second, they rent out equipment to individual clients such as DJs, someone who is organising a birthday party, someone who needs a plasma screen for a trade show or a hotel which needs two flipcharts. Third, they work for projects such as an event, a trade show booth, a party, a concert and yes, once in a while, a meeting.

The average AV company combines all of these very different services in all kinds of different markets and has no real focus. The type of services clients need when they buy equipment for a boardroom is very different from the

services they require in projects such as meetings.
The type of microphones we need for speeches at meetings are very different from the microphone a DJ or singer needs. If an AV company does a meeting, it should use the appropriate meeting microphones. Usually, however, the DJ microphone is used for the speaker desk, leading to all sorts of problems. The AV technician then blames the speaker for not having a good microphone technique while we all know that the speaker is not a professional performer.
Most AV companies never grow bigger than a small, hard-working unit which in many cases just survives and will do anything for anyone while it competes with its neighbouring AV companies.
There is no diploma or certificate needed, so anyone can start an AV company.

Wrong equipment and a lack of focus naturally make most AV companies perform sub-optimally for meetings. If, on top, meeting planners change their AV supplier every time they have a meeting, it becomes difficult to get even the basics right. In such circumstances it is difficult to make meetings improve over time on the content side.

Meetings need and deserve a focused and innovative AV supplier which has all the special kit a meeting needs. Even better is a supplier which combines all the skills and different types of competence a meeting needs – such as creative design, AV, IT, presentation, facilitation, signage, photography, etc.

only long term partners with a focus on meetings and innovation can make a conference grow and prosper

A meeting also needs a long-term relationship with such a supplier in order to gain consistency and stability in the basics. Only then can the meeting improve year on year, building on the previous meeting and keeping participants involved.

Only AV partners with a focus on meetings and innovation combined with a long-term relationship can ensure that a meeting grows and prospers. AV is one part of the content side of meetings where there is clearly room for improvement.

Production companies

Meeting planners for larger conferences will work with a production company or creative agency which in its turn contracts an AV company and other suppliers. Such production companies stage the opening show, produce exciting performances and will create a great experience for the closing night dinner.

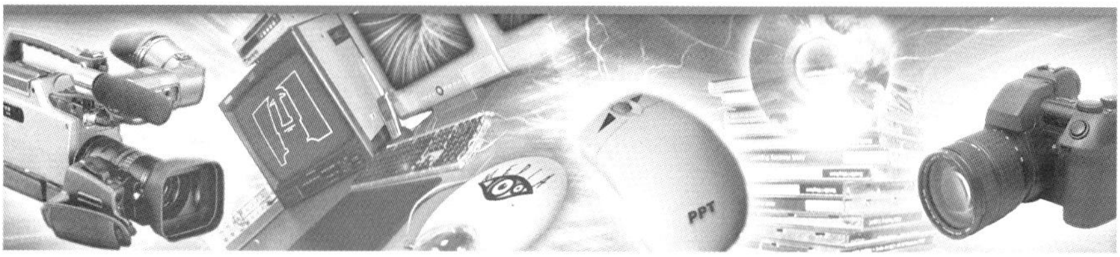

They will create a theme and design and produce creative elements based on the meeting theme. Usually they combine artistes such as dancers with audio-visual productions such as music and video, a light and laser show with a set and stage. Great opening shows have been provided for meetings by wonderfully creative directors. When impressing the audience (motivation) is the key objective of the conference, this is certainly a good way to spend the money. If, however, a conference is mainly educational, secondly networking and only then aims for motivation, one may think twice and reallocate some of the €100,000 that goes into the opening show.

it is “cheap” to spend so much money on one spectacular opening show

It is obvious and very gratifying to create a big wow effect and one could almost say it is “cheap” to spend so much money on one spectacular opening show. Cheap in a way that it is an easy success, just as it is a guaranteed success to book the best hotel and provide the best champagne and food. Everyone knows that it is going to be much more difficult to create a wow with substance than with a show. The industry today knows how the wow factor can be created through exquisite hospitality and a big show. In a way, this makes it vulnerable because this only impacts meetings on the first of five measuring levels towards ROI: satisfaction. See 2 Return on investment on p. 45.

Roughly speaking, we can say that the meeting industry is geared towards the hospitality side and the AV and production company – two partners which could potentially help to develop the content side – are not really helping because of a lack of knowledge and focus.

The WHY Question

Needless to say, the meeting industry wishes to prosper. It wishes to grow, do well, increase its importance and decrease its vulnerability. In order to prosper as an industry, the number one focus must be the clients: the owners of future meetings.
What do they want? They want to meet their objectives and satisfy their clients, the participants. Meeting owners have reasons why they organise meetings: the key objectives. Whoever satisfies those needs or meets those objectives holds the key to success in this industry. If we ask meeting planners the WHY question, they will tell us why their clients organise meetings. The main groups of key objectives of meetings are always the same: Learning, Networking and Motivation for participants. The industry can start to address those and become more than the creator of the environment (the shell) in which someone else addresses the meeting objectives (the substance). If this industry expands its horizons to that arena it may find itself much more wanted in the executive room. Meetings will hold greater strategic importance if they can address the real needs, the key objectives. If the meeting department knows how to identify these key objectives and then designs, executes and measures meetings based on these, it will be seen as crucial to the process. Even with a professional full-time meeting planner, planning the logistics for marketing meetings is perceived as *"only booking a hotel and a few rooms".* Becoming a strategic partner with a real focus and an understanding of the objectives and how to reach them is a different game with a different impact. Co-developing meetings as a strategic revenue generator based on a professional methodology will reduce the "assistant perception" and increase the influence of the industry

Innovation

With its current assets and people, the meetings industry has become truly professional at the hospitality end of the business. The need for specialists, knowledge, tools and concepts to address the key objectives of meetings is clear. Professionals in adult education at meetings, some behavioural psychology for motivation and tools to improve the networking will become instrumental to the industry's next level of success. These companies and individuals are different from the current population in the meetings industry. Many of those companies will also be new to the industry. The meeting industry will have to invite them, welcome them and support them in order to become successful and to ensure they start seeing meetings as their core market.

I have seen many come, get disappointed and leave in the last five years – we need to stop that process and turn it into a positive spiral.

seven innovations per year requires selection

Case: An example of how serious this is, illustrated by the following story. The winner of the technology award for EIBTM in 2004 was a company which specialises in organising and structuring the networking at meetings and events. As far as most meeting planners are concerned, networking is the number two key objective in meetings. One would therefore think that meeting planners would be interested in such an innovation. The winning company was awarded a free stand at the trade show only to conclude after three days that:

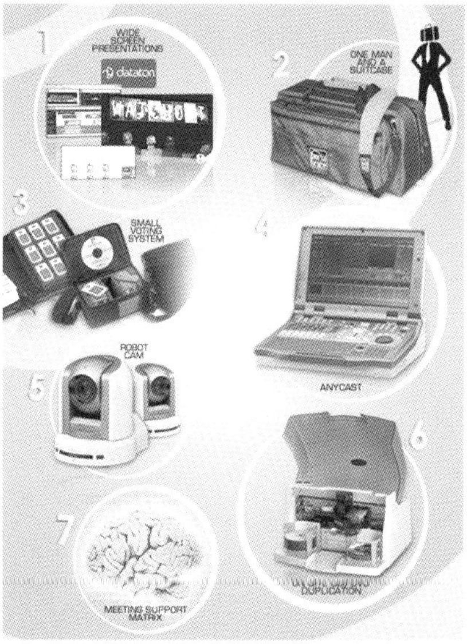

"these people (the meeting planners) are not interested in our product. They have no influence or buying power so this is not our market. Meeting planners are only looking for and maybe deciding on the destination and the venue to have their meeting, not for tools to improve the networking at their meetings."

This is just one of many disappointed companies with tools or services that impact objectives at meetings. If we talk to similar companies which regard the meeting industry as a market for their product, they tell us how frustrated they are when talking to meeting planners. How confusing it is to those newcomers that the meeting planner does not actually plan the meeting but mainly organises the environment in which the meeting takes place.

If the industry could open itself to the content side of meetings and make those companies more welcome, it would change a great deal for the better.

The meeting planner does not actually plan the meeting

Trends supporting change in the industry

Where is the magazine which talks about the content side of meetings? We see only the odd article on technology or learning in the business travel or meeting magazines.
Where is the trade show which gathers together all players on the meetings content side? We get a few stands at the meetings trade show where professional tourism take 98% of the space.
Where is the university where we can get a degree in meeting objectives management rather than a meeting management course that is mainly logistics and hospitality?
These and many other things are clearly missing. The meeting industry is actually like the metal industry calling itself the automotive industry, or the wood industry calling itself the furniture industry.
But what's in a name…

There are three major trends that may help the industry to become more complete and ultimately the rightful claimant of the term Meeting Industry: these trends are Procurement, ROI and Technology.

Procurement

One of the new trends putting pressure on meetings to perform is procurement. Purchasing departments in large corporations have discovered meetings, events and incentives. In some companies the total spend is known and in many cases the procurement people start cutting costs. In many cases they see that a large portion of the meeting spend goes to travel and accommodation – no-one is quantifying income through meetings. They see meetings as a fun activity, a pure cost, not as a revenue generator. Their conclusion could be that some meetings are probably not necessary.

CORPORATE MEETING SPENDING

Hotel	4.8	Hospitality	
Air transportation	6.0	Hospitality	
F&B	4.4	Hospitality	
Production AV	2.0	Meeting Support	10%
Miscellaneous	1.8	Hospitality	
Ground	1.0	Hospitality	
Total	20.0 million US$		100%

Annual spending by a corporate meeting department shows a 10% spend on the content side and 90% on logistics/hospitality.

Since nothing in this example shows the educational effort, the event appears to be an incentive trip rather than a meeting.
Procurement people think in terms of consolidation, standardisation, commodities. And corporate travel managers have been working with procurement for many years. In travel and hotel booking a great deal of consolidation has taken place. Many corporations now know how much they spend on individual travel, hotels and individual flights. They use that to leverage their buying power. If a travel manager consolidates all flights from a multinational and can negotiate about 100,000 tickets, he can surely get some good deals.

Travel executives have had the travel spending well under control for a few years now. Their next logical field of action is meetings and events. This places additional pressure on the planners. The challenge here is that meeting budgets like the one above indicate that a lot can be saved on travel and hospitality. Meeting owners and meeting planners both come under increasing pressure to cut costs. While I believe that in some cases this makes a lot of sense, in other cases it is the over-simplified approach and in most cases a missed opportunity – the opportunity to re-organise the way meetings and conferences are held and being able to turn them into profit centres rather than costs.

Today we are increasingly seeing smaller and smaller teams doing more with less, resulting in even less time for working on the objectives. Managing the content side of meetings will not soon become a commodity. It remains a creative product in which innovation, adaptation, originality and change are the key characteristics. Although this book suggests a standardised way to approach and manage a meeting's objectives, a cookie cutter design or execution will never exist. Rather than dealing with large corporations, HQ to HQ, an individual and trusting client-supplier relationship will remain the norm in this arena.

Return on investment

In 2005 I was part of a focus group for an event magazine. In this group we had event agencies, PCOs, venue owners, and a few corporate meeting planners. The goal was to identify trends in the meeting industry. One of the topics discussed was the Return on Investment (ROI) of meetings and events. How could we keep spending corporate money and not show the value of what we do, the ROI? We will be looked upon as a pure cost if we cannot prove the link between cost and income, between meeting spend and the company's successes.

After this discussion, we had a standing reception with some finger food. And then it happened: at one of the tables, the discussion continued and in the presence of a corporate planner a man from an event agency said: *"We only make sure the event runs smoothly. It is not our job to get the message across or generate Return On Investment."* I was stunned. How could he say that so bluntly and in the presence of a corporate planner? For me, if someone is not interested in the financial result of an event, in the effect it creates, that person should not be involved.

ROI evaluation levels

If we have any interest in this industry we must at least know the five levels of ROI measurement by heart. Based on The European Event ROI Institute and Jack Philips's[2] measuring methodology, there are five levels of

2 *Jack Philips is the Autor of many books and the inventor of the Methodology to measure ROI in Training programs. MPI has worked with Jack Philips to adapt the methodology for meetings and events.*

measuring. Knowing these and accepting them as true is one of the most powerful influences on this industry in this decade

1 SATISFACTION

The lowest level of measuring that most meeting and event planners will perform. Asking the basic question about how good people found the event. Was it impressive? Was it professional? Did we have good food? Did you like the keynote speaker? Etc.
In short, are you satisfied with the event?

2 LEARNING

The second level is somewhat more challenging to measure. It is, however, the next step and without this step we can not go to the following one. In order to be successful, people need to go away with some new knowledge. As far as I'm concerned this can be pure knowledge, but let us also consider the networking – meeting new people such as potential clients, suppliers or peers with whom the participant will do business or collaborate.

3 APPLICATION

The third level of measuring concerns things which arose from the meeting and which participants apply. Is what was learned transferred to application? Do participants use the techniques and knowledge, work differently, etc.? Do they work with the people they met?

4 IMPACT

Once a participant applies what he or she learned, there must be an impact. Are sales growing as a result? Have we raised quality levels? Do we have better inter-departmental collaboration? Are we achieving a higher success rate? Do we have fewer complaints?

5 ROI

The last step one can measure is financial. Every impact on sales or other matters must have a financial impact, generating more income or saving on costs.

When I heard this for the first time in 2004 at MPI's one-day track on ROI with Jack Philips in Denver, Colorado, I thought that this was impossible. Others may also think it impossible. Yes, it is difficult – not impossible but difficult – and it comes at a cost. If you want to learn more about ROI, I can recommend as a first practical step the MPI book on ROI *"Proving the Value of Meetings and Events"* (see bibliography).

We should not measure ROI for every event, but we should do this only once in a while and for the most important meetings we organise

ROI Evaluation Pyramid.

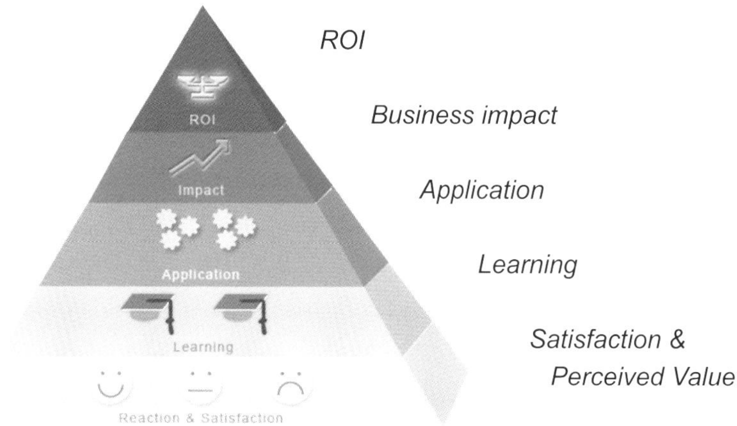

The five levels for measuring ROI in meetings. (Image: European Event ROI Institute)

In short, I see these levels of measuring as a flow: we must have happy (level 1) participants in order to open them to learning (level 2) so that after the meeting they can apply what they learned (3) and thus have an impact (4) on the business that ultimately generates more income or decreases costs (5).
We can not have Impact without the previous step, which is Application. And we can not Apply anything without the step before – Learning. All steps need to be taken in that sequence. Skipping one step will decrease any potential ROI. In that sense it is not simply five levels of measuring, it is also a chain of action in the participant population to be impacted and influenced. The satisfaction (Motivation) and the Learning are the main areas in which we can increase influence at meetings.

This is the opportunity in which Meeting Architecture moves, impacting the content side of meetings will impact its ROI.

ROI all the way?

Today the industry is stretching itself to prove ROI and in doing so creates arguments to counter the cost-cutting movement. It was 9/11 in particular which demonstrated the vulnerability of this industry. Large companies in the meeting industry saw their annual turnover decrease by 30%, 40% and more.

This crisis caused ROI to appear and few will dispute its value. If organising an event does not generate more money than is put into it, we should take a closer look. If an incentive only costs money and does not have any positive financial impact, one should consider investing the money elsewhere – in something which generates better (financial) results. Calculating ROI and proving it convincingly is a complicated and time-consuming matter that most meeting planners and meeting owners will leave to others.
My question in Denver at the end of the ROI course was: "Should we not focus on step two, not just to measure it, but to improve and increase education? Make this industry better and more influential in the learning at the second level, before going all the way up to (just) measuring levels 3, 4 and 5?" The answer I received was that the sense of urgency the industry felt for measuring ROI left us with no time to waste.

ROI driving improvement

generate more ROI

Today I believe ROI measuring methodology is the best thing that happened in a long time. It is one of the key drivers that will steer this industry to its next level. How will that happen?
Let's assume a meeting owner or meeting planner is able to convincingly prove ROI to his board of directors. What will the CFO ask? As an alternative to cutting the budget by 10%, the financial people now have an option: they can ask the meeting planners to increase the ROI! This is the kind of change many meeting planners can only dream of. Instead of decreasing budgets, they now can ask for more resources simply by showing that this will generate more ROI. Meetings now become profit centres in corporations. They are not simply a cost that can be cut in any crisis, but a real opportunity to invest in a strategically important vehicle for corporate success.
Once that change has established itself, the meeting owner or planner is faced with the challenge of increasing ROI. In order to increase ROI (5) one needs to enlarge the Impact (4) that is based on the Application (3) of what participants Learned (2) because they were in the right mood (1)

From measuring to action

If we take a closer look at the five levels of measuring ROI, there are actually several where meeting professionals can increase their impact. Making the participant more satisfied (1) and making the learning (2) better are things we can do, not just measure. And that is obviously the next thing that will have to happen as a consequence of ROI being measured.

1	SATISFACTION	Direct impact by the meeting organiser	Actionable
2	LEARNING		
3	APPLICATION	Secondary impact, after the meeting	
4	IMPACT	No impact	Measurable
5	ROI		

Put simply, more satisfied participants will learn more and so will be able to apply more and have more impact, thus generating more ROI.

Levels one and two are actionable: we can impact those in many ways at meetings and events. There are hundreds of things one can do to improve the learning curve at conferences. Level three we may impact by organising post event follow up activities.

This is why measuring ROI is driving the industry's attention towards the content side of meetings; simply because if content is managed better for more ROI, meeting budgets will be under less pressure.

Technology

The final driving force for increasing attention to the content side of meetings is technology. Things change rapidly and every week a new product is launched with a potential impact on the learning, networking or motivational objectives at meetings.

These new and innovative companies are entering the meetings industry with more and more success. They start to advertise, participate in trade shows, speak at conferences. This technology simply becomes more visible and provides the meeting planner with options for increasing influence on the content side of meetings.

One level up

The meetings industry can move from being a cost into a profit centre of strategic relevance. As an industry, it needs to make some bold and strategic decisions. It needs to open up its horizons and vote for some radical innovation. This will require out-of-the-box thinking and some drastic innovation. Moving the industry one level up from where it is today will require a mind shift in thousands of individuals, a paradigm shift in many established institutions.

Conferences involving the meeting industry itself should not just educate about planning meetings but educate about improving education in meetings. In short, a conference about conferences which educates about education, meta-education.

the Meeting Content Conference (Frankfurt, 2007) was a meeting with education about education for meetings

Magazines should not just have an article on how I, as a reader, can network better at meetings but also on how I, as a planner, can help all participants at my meetings to achieve more effective networking. Meeting planners should be able to design and implement networking elements in meetings that establish exactly the specific kind of networking that a particular meeting audience needs.

Meeting associations should not just have an award for marketing events but also an award for how events support the marketing objectives of an organisation.

meta-education

Based on this industry's current strength in hospitality, the hospitality players will be required to support and maybe even drive that next-level-process, which will ultimately improve the industry as a whole.

Comwell, a hotel chain in Denmark is a pioneer in that field. Lotte Marie Roesgaard is the Comwell HR manager and she is one of the driving forces. She spoke at MPI's PEC-Europe in 2007 and is quoted in the MPI White Paper *"Mapping the future of on-site learning"*. Comwell currently trains its staff in meeting design and wants them to understand and be involved in the design side of meetings.

Comwell Meeting Designer is a trademark they use and the goal is to teach their conference managers how to approach meetings and meeting planning differently. Rather than executing only what a meeting planner asks, they will now also ask questions on the objectives and offer different solutions in designing the meeting for their clients. Hotel conference managers have always been service-minded people who tend to say yes to every request from clients, no questions asked.

The internal course helps hotel conference managers reach a level of confidence, so these professionals now dare ask important questions about the purpose of the meeting. Rather than focusing only on the logistics support a hotel can give, they now try to help by looking at, learning about and offering assistance for what happens inside meetings. The internal Comwell courses teach about facilitation, meeting formats like Open Space and the Learning Meeting (see the book by Steen Elsborg, Ib Ravn People's Press 2006). They keep Comwell conference coordinators up to speed on the latest tools and methods that can provide answers to a customer's questions about how to activate participants. Scandinavian countries have always had a strong sense of democracy and the younger generation wants more of that in meetings as well. Comwell staff will offer guidance to customers and bases a lot of its knowledge on the science of education. Concepts such as physical activity to support education is based on research from schools.

In the early stages it was somewhat challenging to approach a customer with that concept. Many found these questions awkward and strange. But with the development of flowcharts for phone conversations and other tools, they managed to find the approach that leads to success. The main result is that clients come back and their numbers show a growth in a time that the market was declining. Lotte Marie says:

"In 2006 our turnover in Sweden went up by 4% in a market that in general was going down. Our Swedish hotel managers attributed this to our Meeting Designer concept. In Denmark it is not so easy to contribute progress primarily to the concept. However we see that our costumer reviews have improved and customers regularly comment on how we have helped them improve their meetings…"

And more is happening in the Scandinavian countries. Lars Blicher-Hansen from visitdenmark.com is head of event tourism. They have a project called "Danish Meetings" and this also approaches the market via the meeting objectives. They are leading the way and show that the hospitality side of the meeting industry can benefit from in developing the content side of the industry.

Strategic Meeting Management

For many years the word strategic has been a buzz word in the meeting industry. I once went to an educational session on strategic meeting management where the facilitator asked participants what it meant. Again to my surprise, the only elements people would state were all about general strategic business issues such as procurement, finance, budgeting, security, standardised contracts, strategic partnerships with hotel brands, etc. Obviously these things are important and even crucial depending on the type and size of the organisation, but I was still expecting to hear people talk about alignment with the corporate brand and communication strategy, efforts to help set the meeting's objectives, methodologies for increasing the meeting's effects, etc. Again the session was fully focused on the logistics of meetings and not on the substance or the objectives. Just like my visit to the trade show at the end of the 1990s, it was now 2005 and I still felt somewhat alienated in an industry that seemed to overlook the essence of its own existence.

Another example is the CMM programme. I did my CMM with MPI in 2004. CMM is a Certification in Meeting Management and is all about strategic thinking and working. I enjoyed the five-day residential course and the progress towards a strategic plan after the course which ultimately led to certification. The course and the certificate are all about the strategic side of general business practices such as marketing, communication, negotiation, etc.; all important presentations and great speakers, leading to a very valuable certificate but not to more knowledge about the essence of meetings, their objectives. (The industry also has the widespread CMP – Certification for Meeting Professionals – which is geared towards meeting logistics and is a more operational meeting logistics certificate.)

> an industry that overlooks the essence of its own existence

My dream is that the industry instates a similar programme for the content side of meetings, a programme in which senior meeting planners can learn about the Learning in presentations, network around Networking in conferences and get motivated about Motivation for meeting participants. For me, this is of strategic importance not only for meetings, but for the entire industry. Senior meeting planners today have a choice of becoming strategic in several ways: leading a team of meeting planners, moving into procurement or even moving away from the industry into marketing or other management positions. Would it not be a valuable fourth option for many senior meeting professionals to specialise in the content side of meetings? Helping meeting owners with the substance instead of the shell and driving the content, supporting the key objectives. It could be a stepping stone towards a more strategic position in the corporations but also a potential career goal for a meeting professional.

The industry would retain many meeting professionals in the industry itself rather than losing them to corporate management.

Conclusion about the meetings industry

The meeting industry today is in a very natural way immersed in, developed by and controlled by the tourism industry. This travel and hospitality side of the meeting industry (a.k.a. the shell) is professional, global, well organised and has a number of large multinational players. This is a good thing and its strength allows the current industry to choose to take ownership of meeting content too (a.k.a. the substance) and develop the industry further. This second leg is clearly important to meeting owners but is also under-developed and not organised. With the potential of completing the meeting industry with its second leg, this can cause the industry to move on to a thriving future. Rather than just measuring ROI, the meeting professional's objective should be about driving, creating and increasing ROI. This takes us to the real core of the business – learning and motivation.

Developing the content side is the biggest opportunity this industry can find.

5. Meeting Content

Definition

Meeting content is everything that happens 'inside' a particular meeting and is directly based on that meeting's objectives.

Meeting content is not simply the educational content of presentations. It is much more! The presentation content based on the knowledge of experts is part of a conference's main topic and as such is certainly part of meeting content. Selecting the topics and speakers is a task that meeting planners and in some cases professional development (PD) specialists cover. Meeting content, however, covers a much wider range of matters in not only educational goals, but also networking and motivational goals. Meeting content is ideally a well-analysed and detailed list of all objectives for a meeting.

In that sense, meeting content is the raison d'être of meetings. Meeting content is why meetings are organised in the first place and is therefore critical to the meeting industry – without meeting content there is no need for meetings. No logistics are necessary, no venues needed, there is no travel to a destination – therefore there are no grounds for a meeting industry to exist. Luckily for all of us, these reasons are present, at least in the minds of a number of people who keep organising meetings.

meeting content is the raison d'être of meetings

It would seem logical for an industry to get a grip on the existential reasons for that industry. It's like the oil and the automotive industries: there's no need for the oil if cars don't use it. Cars are the reason for the existence of the oil industry. It is probably safe to say that if the oil industry is well connected to the automotive industry it has more influence on its own existence. In the same way, the meeting hospitality industry would be smart to become well connected to the meeting content industry. The challenge is that there is no such industry. The opportunity exists in that we can create it.

Why meetings

When asking meeting planners what they consider the key objectives of meetings, I pose this simple question: Why do you or your clients organise meetings? These are the kind of answers we get:

Brainstorming, education, learning, refreshing knowledge, training, communicating message, product launch, planning, changing behaviour, information gathering, crisis solving, creating new strategy, promotion, advocacy, publishing procedures, problem solving, strategy development, innovation. Networking, visibility, exchanging ideas, meeting new clients, meeting new suppliers, making industry friends, completing my network of partners, interacting, fun, celebrating, incentive, awards, motivation, involving people, team building, team spirit, sense of community, experience…

At present I have gathered some 200 distinct words which meeting planners consider key objectives for meeting participants. Many of those words mean the same thing or something similar. Some are broad and some are very specific. It's a list, a long one, and it demonstrates the wealth of good reasons for organising meetings or conferences. Interestingly enough, hospitality is almost never given as a reason. No-one says they organise meetings so they can travel, although travelling is a necessity for international conferences. No-one says they organise meetings in order to be able to arrange nice lunches and dinners for a group, although we all know these things are fundamental.

After gathering the real reasons behind meetings a few times with the groups of planners, I began to see three distinct groups in the list; groups of participant objectives which I would call "terrains of action". Each terrain requires our distinct attention and allows for a different set of actions a meeting organiser could deploy in order to reach his or her objectives.

These three terrains are Learning, Networking and Motivation. When we sort out the earlier list of words, the list of key objectives, all should fit into at least one of these terrains. Some have an overlap and some fit partially in each but every meeting objective fits into at least one.

Learning
Brainstorming, education, learning, refreshing knowledge, training, exchanging ideas, communicating message, product launch, planning, information gathering, crisis solving, creating new strategy, promotion, advocacy, publishing procedures, problem solving, strategy development, innovation.

Networking
Meeting new clients, meeting new suppliers, making industry friends, starting a network, visibility, completing my network of partners, interacting.

Motivation
Fun, celebrating, incentive, awards, motivation, involving people, team building, team spirit, changing behaviour, sense of community, experience.

These three groups cover everything and are the first step in an holistic approach to meeting content management or Meeting Architecture. Some individuals will focus on learning and include networking as a way of learning. I think that learning is the most important part but it is not the whole picture.

Some books and speakers will defend Networking as the unique aspect of meetings, but again this is not the only thing. Other companies will emphasise totally the wow experience which fits the Motivational terrain, and again, spending all our money and attention there is in most cases a mistake.

Paying attention to all three and finding the right balance for our conference is crucial.

Learning, Networking and Motivation connected to ROI methodology

If we look back to the five levels of measuring ROI (p. 47) we see some similarities. Motivation is level one: Satisfaction. Satisfaction is a state of mind. It is a rather technical way of saying that people are in a good mood. Motivation is more result oriented – being motivated to be open to the content of the presentation, but also leaving the conference motivated for action, for change in behaviour, etc. So that is our level one. But here it is a terrain of activities, a part of the meeting to focus on.
Level two is clear: Education is learning = level two. In meetings and conferences this is clearly the most important objective and the one where we are able gain the most impact since it is such an underdeveloped field.

Between levels 1 Motivation and 2 Learning from the ROI measuring model, I have added networking. Networking clearly appeared as the second key objective in meetings and conferences. Networking is a distinct terrain where different tools and methods apply, where meeting organisers could invest in specific support. Networking also fits very neatly between Education and Motivation because it influences and overlaps with both. For example, learning from and sharing with other participants (peer to peer learning) is a way of networking that is fun (ROI level 1) and educational (ROI level 2)

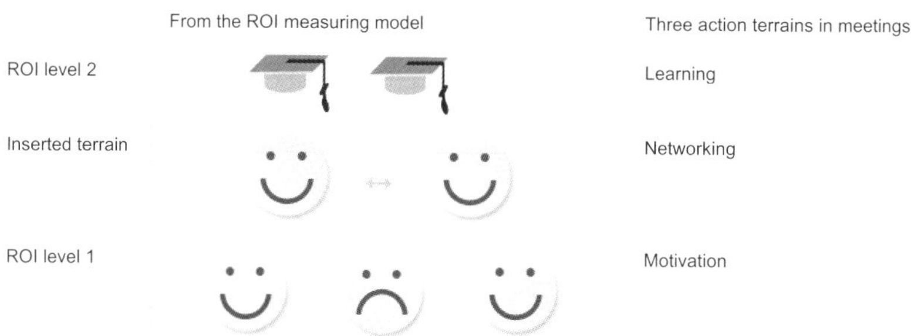

The list of meeting objectives indicates that Networking, like Motivation and Learning, is an action terrain for meetings.

In this chapter, these three groups of key objectives will be further developed and analysed, and finally result in a basic tool for analysing meeting objectives called the Meeting Objective Matrix®. This is useful material for anyone involved in analysing the goals and objectives of meetings. It provides a simple structure that offers guidance and clarity to an otherwise chaotic and incomplete process.

Learning

The first things that come to mind when we talk about learning at meetings are presentations. Many conferences are built around experts who present their knowledge. This, of course, is important but there is so much more to learning. In *"Learning Meetings and Conferences in Practice",* a book by Steen Elsborg and Ib Ravn, (People's Press, 2006) you will find that such presentations are

more time for written reflection

part of any meeting but in many cases should be shorter and create space for more reflection, discussion and interaction around the presented topic. Presentations should be short, to the point and provide discussion material. The presented research shows that meeting participants learn much more from each other when given the opportunity. This provides us with two learning dimensions: learning from the expert and learning from other participants. In other words, top down and horizontal education. I would add a third learning dimension: bottom up education. This occurs when the organisation or company learns from its conference participants. Clearly in these circumstances, the audience has now become a group of participants and this change is a trend that currently takes many shapes and forms.

An example: MPI's PEC-NA was themed 'Meet Different', and after Mary Boone's presentation there, I looked up the article she mentioned from BusinessWeek about 'Unconference'. There is a whole industry out there that is starting to change the way conferences are conducted. This article confirms we should make meetings more interactive, fun, educational, open and all the positive characteristics of web 2.0 that young people have come to expect from life. The unconference 'movement' is part of a growing group of formats that real meeting professionals can choose from to design (parts of) their meetings – formats such as the Learning Meeting, Open Space, Pecha Kucha, Wiki Workshops, etc. These enable conference organisers to add essential moments of interactivity, involvement, democracy, crowd sourcing, reflection and fun. And yes, most conferences today can do with some of that.
Mary Boone is a leadership and collaboration consultant who represents an industry we need to welcome because its knowledge and business techniques can enrich the learning, networking and motivational aspects in meetings.

Crowd sourcing

The book *"Wisdom of Crowds"* by James Surowiecky (Abacus, 2005) talks about the power and importance of groups and how smart and surprisingly accurate predictors groups of individuals can be. This book is a "must read" for anyone involved in organising meetings. The book uses various stories, cases and research to demonstrate something that is very applicable in meetings – exciting stories about how a group of people was able to pinpoint a sunken submarine in a vast ocean, and how group talk made the Challenger explode on its return to the Earth's atmosphere. Learning as a company or an organisation from participants is, in most meetings, an untapped resource. It is a simple and fun thing to do and when done well can provide information that can mean the difference between good and great for organisations.

Think about how a meeting always brings together participants who are experts in one area and what an immense concentration of knowledge there is in one room... How powerful would it be if we could connect all participants to a brain hub linked to a knowledge server that downloads, sorts, analyses, summarises and shares the knowledge of all participants. If we imagine a software user group, how valuable would it be if we could quickly and efficiently get all the ideas from all participants, all comments – good and bad – listed and sorted in one session at our meeting...

This is actually possible. It is just not done a lot and most meeting organisers do not know the methods to apply, the tools or technology to use or the companies and facilitators who do that for a living. Crystal Interactive is such a company (www.meetingsupport.org). Many meeting organisers do not even consider it because they have never heard of it. They don't look for it because they don't know what they don't know.

If presentations are top-down education and discussion is horizontal learning or peer to peer learning, then the third direction is "bottom up" and it completes the educational scope of directions.

connect all participants to a brain hub

linked to a knowledge server

Full circle education

Top-Down education	Lecture, presentation from an expert or panel of experts to the audience	The classic format. Every conference has a lot of this. Most conferences have only this.
Horizontal education	A.ka. peer to peer education. Participants learning from each other, sharing best practices, etc.	In most meetings this is just a short Q&A and the rest happens during random networking at coffee or lunch breaks.
Bottom-Up education	Aka crowd sourcing: Collecting participants' ideas and comments for the group or the organiser.	This is probably the most powerful educational stream. Almost no-one uses it except for voting systems (ARS) which don't provide rich, text-based information.

full circle education at meetings enables a rich and full educational experience which keeps adults awake and involved

These are different learning directions that can take place individually but which we have combined all in one learning experience. This is also a good order:

- First, have an expert speak on new or controversial issues.
- Second, have the group talk among themselves.
- Third, collect feedback from the group.

We can add a repeat of the horizontal learning (discussion) before going to the next presentation to complete the circle.

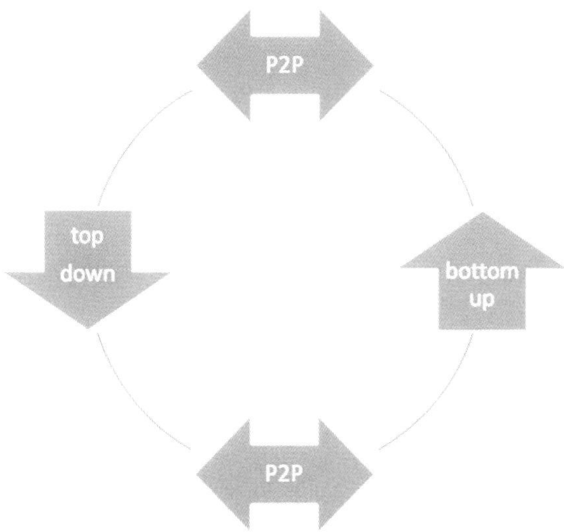

the 360° learning cycle starts with the presentation (top down) then group discussions (peer to peer) followed by feedback (bottom up) etc

A great number of books have been published about education, fewer about adult education and even fewer about adult education at meetings and conferences. One such book on meetings and learner objectives is "Objectives to Outcomes: Your Contract With the Learner" (Glen C. Ramsborg, 1995) and is certainly worth reading. It presents existing learning techniques and translates these for the meeting industry. One piece of theory is about the levels in the "cognitive domain". The learning starts with knowledge then comprehension followed by application. The higher levels are the ability to analyse, synthesise and evaluate. Some of this probes deeper into the cognitive world which is mainly uncharted territory for the meetings industry.

Similar books can be found in the online knowledge base of the Meeting Support Institute (See p. 99).

I don't remember where I heard it

One of the bigger challenges in learning and meetings is that we have a hard time remembering where we learned or heard something for the first time. In other words, it is difficult to demonstrate the connection between one individual going to conferences and the knowledge he or she acquired there. In some cases it is only having the same information repeated, perhaps on different occasions, that causes it to sink in, stick and ultimately change behaviour. It is much easier to remember a few impressive visual moments we link with a destination or a hotel and the conference.

Of course I remember the palm tree swinging wildly during a hurricane in Miami at the last MPI conference there. I even remember one or two people I was at the bar with drinking a cocktail when this storm happened. I have no recollection whatsoever about what sessions I went to at that conference let alone about what I learned there. Lots of information and even things I do today were, however, acquired by me at that conference. I just can not tell you what they are. This is a big challenge for the industry. Measuring level two (learning) and three (applying) in the ROI measurement method will help us understand the educational results.

I do remember some sessions I have been to as well as some of the learning from those sessions and even apply it. I remember the speaker, the topic and what I learned there, but now I can't tell you at which conference it was.

I remember, for example, a session with Robin Lokerman from MCI about a window/mirror metaphor. He explained in a session about 'working with staff' that credit for successes needs to be shared – through the window – with the team, while failure needs to be seen as the leader's own doing – looking in the mirror. I'm trying to remember where this session was, but I can't decide which of 15 possible conferences it was. The good thing is that I remember this was a session at a conference; the sad thing is that I don't have recollection of the source of a lot of other things I know and do. As a result it is difficult to make a reasonable estimation of the educational value of all those conferences I once went to.

research

Research in that terrain and a resulting method to examine and demonstrate educational output in individual participants would clearly leverage the meeting industry. Even if we don't measure or don't know the exact educational impact of conferences, we know that education is a stepping stone to ROI – improving it will improve ROI. And there is a lot we can do to improve education at conferences, or even before and after the event itself. Some concepts and ideas are just free of charge or you could rent services from companies which, for example, provide computers, software and facilitation to really impact the horizontal and bottom-up learning. There are a few hundred items, both large and small, we could apply to our conference in order to make participants learn more, share more, remember more.

Levels of activity in learning

Besides the top-down, horizontal and upwards education, there is also the activity differentiation: Passive, Reactive, Active, Interactive, Collaborative, Co-creative. For a few years now the interactive buzz has been around. Most of us will understand what this means. Interactivity in meetings is hot, mainly because many meetings are perceived as boring. As a counter-measure to participants falling asleep, interactivity sounds just right. Most meeting owners are in favour of more interactivity and any solution will do as long as the audience does not fall asleep. A lot of interactivity is generated by including a Q&A a few minutes long after each presentation. But is Q&A really interactivity? I would accept it is clearly not passive: a question from a participant is at least a reaction to the presentation. And since there is an answer from the speaker,

standing co-creation with a laptop: no sleeping here (Photo Holliday Inn)

we may call it active too. For many Q&As, however, the term interactive is an overstatement. Interactivity in meetings would imply to me that the audience and the speaker or panel become involved in reflection and discussion. The same goes for voting systems, which are a great tool. But I would prefer to call these reactive, as the audience reacts to a question by clicking a keypad button. Voting systems generate a lot of valuable information for the speaker and the meeting owner. They clearly involve the audience and can even give participants some decision-making power (motivational) depending on the types of question. If applied, for example, to decide where the next meeting will take place or who the audience prefers as the next keynote speaker, then it obviously becomes an interactive tool. In most cases, however, meeting owners don't go that far so it remains more of a reactive model.

co-creation and collaboration

Other new buzz words are co-creation and collaboration. These are about working with participants to create something new at a meeting. In this way participants learn from each other and the organisation also learns from the group. This is based on web 2.0 and its current success of blogs and Wikis where many individuals create and control the content via online communities. I would like to call a meeting that focuses totally on this aspect of co-creation a Wiki workshop. A Wiki workshop could start online with a selection of participants using online software such as Synthetron to create a list of topics for the conference. During the meeting, Open Space as described in the book *"Open Space Technology"* (Harrison, 1977), could be the format to use for co-creation. A Wiki or another online community application could be used for taking notes and keeping the co-creation going after the meeting.

Learning or Education is the number one objective of most meetings. The above few pages introduced very briefly the complexity and variety of learning at meetings. The second key objective for most meetings is Networking.

Networking

A large medical conference of some 8,000 participants takes place in South Africa. A whole group of participants become sick and as the illness is contagious are confined to their hotel rooms. The conference-goers are stuck for a few days but two of them accidentally meet in the lobby and start talking. This is a random encounter: they have never met before, but they seem to be interested in the same topic. The conversation continues in the elevator where they decide to have a drink in one of their rooms. The therapeutic area they work in is the same, but their disciplines and skills are complementary. They end up lunching and dining together and spend the whole conference sharing ideas and discussing matters, just the two of them. Back home they stay in touch and soon start a scientific research project together. The project's results are published widely and recognised as one of the most important studies in that therapeutic area. About 50 other research projects have started based on their research.

Remember, two individuals met only because both were ill and were staying in the same hotel.
They spent some intense and long networking time together because they had nothing else to do. A number of unplanned reasons created the connection which today influences or even saves the lives of thousands. I call that the power of random encounters. This is one of the most powerful results of conferences and is precisely why meetings will never be replaced by video conferencing or virtual meetings.
Video conferencing means we will usually have small groups of people who know each other. The chance of a random encounter is therefore limited. Building a trusting relationship takes more than seeing a face on a screen and hearing a voice. It needs bonding practices such as shaking hands and sharing food to set off a neurological process that generates powerful substances in the old part of the brain, making the bonding process stronger.

No $E=MC^2$ without conference networking

I also believe that people meeting people, and especially specialists meeting specialists, lies at the basis of any innovation. Einstein would never have developed his relativity theory without having met other scientists who understood, challenged and fuelled every step he took to get to $E= MC^2$.

Albert Einstein met Marie Curie at a conference in Brussels, organised by Solvay in 1911. They spoke and had lunch or dinner together. What learning and motivation took place during that conference I don't know, but it is safe to assume that some of it made the young Einstein's thinking move forward. With a little imagination we can even see an exhausted Einstein being coached by the much older Marie Curie and put back on track.

What precisely happened there is not important. What is important is the assumption that progress in this world mainly occurs because one individual meets and talks to a range of diverse people with similar interests at meetings and conferences.

networking with electronic badges (photo nTag)

If we understand the value and importance of networking and accept the potential of random encounters or accidental meetings, how about paying some attention to it at our conferences? How about trying to organise real networking moments rather than just hoping that networking will take place during lunch? How about even structuring the networking, so we make sure that the high potential in a mix of people is actually realised? Or even putting individuals together based on an automated system which matches people based on high-value networking potential?

We could also use techniques or technology to facilitate the networking. This could involve allowing participants to select their targets themselves based on available information and radar-based (existing) pocket technology which warns them when they are close and even shows a picture to help them find each other.

The middle position

The fact that Networking is positioned between Learning and Motivation (see p. 58) is not a coincidence. The Networking actually has a connection with both Learning and Motivation. When you network with your peers you learn a lot from them. Some formats include lots of discussion for peer-to-peer learning and call it networking. If you meet new people you have access to new knowledge. In many cases, building a network of people is building a resource for future information. Networking is also very motivational since you make friends, you share, you meet people with the same professional interests etc. This is why it is positioned between Learning and Motivation – it actually results in both.

handheld device for networking (Photo Spotme)

The fact that it is seen as a separate terrain is because there are a lot of potential actions that will specifically stimulate networking during a conference. These actions are different from educational ones. Supporting networking at meetings needs a separate focus. It needs time and attention from the organising team in order to function optimally. There are separate tools such as Spotme, N-Tag and Badge2match to connect people, as well as software-based tools like Converve which purely focus on introducing people-based on information from participant profiles. Services such as the RFID-based system from Mercurius RFID Solutions automatically introduce each individual who walks into a room and shows a picture and name from a database. People in the room see that person enter on the screen and can actively meet up if they wish (see www.meetingsupport.org member list). In addition to tools such as these from Meeting Support Institute members, there is also an amount of knowledge to be uncovered – how introverts network, for example. They are a majority and don't feel comfortable in a roomful of strangers. An article on this topic can be found on the Meeting Support Institute website knowledge base.

There are many different kinds of networking and networking goals:

NETWORKING	Random	Stimulated	Organised
Social			
Peer to Peer			
Business			

This table lists the main categories of networking at meetings.

These and more aspects of networking should be discussed and analysed in order to understand the full scope of needed, desired and nice-to-have networking: the networking objectives.
Don't forget that networking can start before the conference and needs to be supported after the conference in order to really raise its impact value.
After learning, networking is one of three key objectives in meetings. As with learning, networking is an action terrain. It holds a place of influence which needs specific attention and it drives results for meetings.

Perfect Motivation

The Motivational aspect of the meeting is the third and final group of objectives. This is an area most participants will not mention as a reason for going to a conference. From the organisers' perspective, however, we can see it is important. A participant will not say that the conference is a way of staying motivated in his or her job.
One conference organiser once mentioned to me, however, that their annual conference was "therapy" for their participants. This conference is the ASAP conference – the Association of Strategic Alliance Professionals Conference. Strategic alliance professionals have a job not many know about. They are alone in most cases and feel unrecognised in their respective companies. Participating in their ASAP conference where they meet peers and discuss and share common issues is a powerful medication for their professional isolation. At the conference they feel part of a group, a tribe, which again is a very old and basic human need. Small things such as an opening video or photography make them feel that someone is taking good care of them.

the conference as therapy

Obviously there is also the motivational connection to the hospitality side of a conference. A nice trip to an attractive destination and a stay in a good hotel with wonderful meals also creates that positive and motivational feeling. This travel and hospitality side is, as mentioned before, the side that is well established and therefore not addressed in this book. The kind of motivation which we feel needs to be addressed and increased at meetings is the part that fits the content side, the key objectives of a meeting or conference.

The perfect formula

Since motivation is so important everything that impacts on it should be perfect. At the same time PERFECT is another acronym that applies to the motivational aspects of meetings.
The most important categories in motivation for participants are:

Professional, Expertise, Respect, Fun, Evaluation, Connection and Tying = PERFECT

Professional

This is about doing all the educational, networking and motivational work at meetings in a professional way. Getting the basics right is step number one. But all other things need to be done well too, with the help of professionals to ensure everything takes place on an appropriate level. Participants come a long way and don't wish to spend their valuable time confronted with amateur work. This does not mean every meeting has to be a big show, but whatever takes place should be well prepared and executed in a flawless way. Amateurism is a great way to lower motivation levels quickly and hinder results. At meetings it is better to do less but do it well than it is to do more but execute it poorly. The audience is a dragon with 200 heads and is accordingly difficult to please.

Expertise

When specialists come to your meeting they want to learn from the best. Getting the experts on stage is crucial to fulfilling the desired outcome. The effort needed to get the right people can challenge resources, but that should be exceptional. A meeting owner must get the best possible speakers on any given topic. This is an under-estimated task which takes more effort than can usually be spent. It also clearly influences education. But the presence of the real experts or the well known opinion leaders also has that motivational effect. I, as a participant, feel more important as a result of it.

Respect

wiki workshop: respect through crowd sourcing

Respect for the participant is crucial. This is a no-brainer. More specifically, a meeting needs to respect the knowledge and value of each participant. Besides having experts on stage, conferences must provide a significant amount of time for discussion, interaction, expression, etc. Crowd sourcing, wisdom of crowds, re-conference, Open Space, Wiki workshops and many other formats help to create that kind of participant respect. Tools such as voting and collaboration systems also support this objective.

Fun

During the meeting itself, fun is a formidable force. Many of our participants work and live at a fast pace and are used to a high level of activity through mobiles, laptops, text messages, etc. The opportunity to become passive is something they might love during a beach holiday but not necessarily at a conference. Being active and involved will be much more appealing than a full day of hour long speeches. Using a variety of media, tools and techniques for presentations and learning will be much more appealing and fun than all-day PowerPoint. Fun can be built in in many ways and should be considered a means of keeping people awake and focused during the various stages of a meeting. The first things we think of in order to add fun are to provide entertainment during the dinner or to provide outdoor, sports and other activities. These are of course an option, but building the fun in the meeting itself makes a lot of sense too, especially at a time when regulations and ethics are increasingly challenging fun activities.

Evaluation

One of the better ways of keeping participants motivated is to test how much they remember from a session as soon as it ends. In some instances meeting owners are not comfortable testing their participants, but an exam can be kept anonymous. It could be part of the programme book and kept private by the participant. Once a participant realises that tests are taken, focus and attention will increase. Evaluating the participant's learning outcomes as a motivator works. Research has demonstrated this clearly (see article on www.meetingsupport.org knowledge base).

Continuation

Ensuring that a number of activities are lined up in the months after a meeting is a good thing too. It reminds participants about their presence and certainly works as a motivator for applying what was learned and for attending again next year.

Tying

Tying happens in the weeks before the next conference and at the beginning of the next conference. The key messages or, even better, conclusions from last year's meeting, are reinforced. The participant realises that the previous year's meeting was not forgotten and that the work participants did during the meeting was not in vain.

Make the meeting part of a series. If possible set a long-term goal and design a long term theme. Every meeting then also focuses on the long-term objective and the theme varies only according to the current phase of the long-term project (see also Dirk Reyn meetings on p. 18).

This palette of diverse motivational aspects is a shortlist of things to think about during the design phase of meetings. Brainstorming around these elements will lead to many other ideas arising. These may be more appropriate for the project in hand.

Nobody asks to be motivated

When we ask meeting organisers why they organise a meeting many answers are about motivation. When we ask participants the same question almost no one will tell us that they come to get motivated.

At the end of a conference many will say they feel their batteries have been recharged and that they feel re-energised. But no-one comes to a conference because they feel they need to be recharged. Obviously, spending a few days out of the office and returning with charged batteries sounds like a good investment, and one that is not for the sales team alone.

The three terrain formula

In the previous pages we looked at the three key elements which make up meeting content learning, networking and motivation. These represent three groups of meeting objectives. For a meeting owner, these are three terrains for action, the three terrains where a meeting planner can make things happen, where he or she can drive objectives etc.

Knowing that the actual application of what is learned drives the ROI of meetings. It is the motivation to act that can make all the difference. The importance of motivation at meetings is emphasised in this formula:

(Learning + Networking) x Motivation = Meeting Result

Motivation in this case is not motivation to attend the conference. It is motivation to take action on what was learned and to continue to build relationships that were started at the conference. This will boost the results at level 3 of measuring: Application. As converting Learning to Application occurs after the meeting, some motivation may also be needed after the meeting. This can be organised by the meeting team. Surveying or even asking about application a few weeks and a few months after the conference helps participants to move to the next crucial step. Motivation and repeated support are needed to drive participants out of their routines and really change behaviour.

PERFECT Motivation: some examples and results

Category	Examples	Results in
PROFESSIONALISM	Getting the basics right on the content side of meetings is in many cases a challenge. For example, if meeting rooms do not have a technician, which still occurs a lot, speakers are alone when they start their presentation. An already nervous speaker's performance does not get any better if a session starts with technical problems. With professionally developed and supported presentations the participant feels taken care of as an intellectual individual	Pride, sense of belonging, retention
EXPERTISE	Credibility of speakers, innovation, market leadership, positive news,	Learning, believing, application, advocacy, teaching
RESPECT FOR PARTICIPANT	Allowing every participant to contribute and to express opinions is showing respect to them as knowledgeable individuals. Video interviews for the closing video, voting systems and many other means help the participant to feel respected	Respect, more open and giving atmosphere, co-creation, sense of belonging
FUN	Creative meeting concepts, variation, games, quizzes, technology, etc. all contribute to a level of fun. Using drama, actors, entertainment during presentations helps to create a fun experience. Wow effects. Organised networking…	Better collaboration, interaction, sharing
EVALUATION	Test, examine, reflection, survey	More attention, more learning, higher retention
CONTINUATION	Keep the meeting and its messages alive after the meeting. Repeat, remind, certification	More learning, greater appreciation, more attention to the next meeting
TIE	Connect this meeting from and to the previous and following ones. Ensure people see that annual meetings connect and are built on. If possible create a long-term goal for a series of meetings	More credibility, sense of importance, mandate

The Motivation table is PERFECT – the seven main categories in the motivational arena at meetings.

Motivation in hospitality

What is also clear is that the hospitality side of the motivation coin plays a key role. It plays a vital role in level one measuring (see ROI evaluation levels p. 47), the reasoning being that if a person does not feel happy with the hospitality not much will be learned. This means that to achieve good adult learning, appropriate hospitality is a must.

Fulfilling the intellectual needs of a group of people at meetings is at least as challenging as fulfilling their bodily needs such as eating, drinking, sleeping, etc. However, there is no industry, trade show, conference or formal education that focuses on the intellectual zone.

There are hundreds of places we can go for a great meal in every capital, but where do we find someone to prepare a decent meal to satisfy the mental hunger? There are dozens of hotel chains we can rely on to perform to standard and make the hospitality side run smoothly, but where do we look for the meeting-focused team which will facilitate the networking? Where do we find the specialist who will combine all the right creative, technical and technological ingredients into a wonderful mix that meets the pre-determined conference objectives?

Most chefs are well aware of all the available ingredients they can work with in their kitchens, but how many of us know all the potential ingredients that will create motivation during a meeting? There are no global brands to choose from, no major chains to rely on. A step in that direction is the creation of the profession of Meeting Architect.

Meeting Objectives Matrix®

The Meeting Objectives Matrix® is a simple one-page document that helps in the first phase of developing a good meeting.
It shows the three terrains of key objectives and lists all potential objectives for meetings
It helps teams of people organising a meeting to discuss and brainstorm in an organised way and assists them to see possibilities that were unseen before
It is all about investigating and analysing the key objectives before starting to design the meeting

If an organisation allows a professional to help in that phase, some out-of-the-box thinking will occur and the potential of the meeting will be explored and expanded.

Many meetings are organised with only a few objectives or even just the one. Spending time identifying ALL objectives with a multidisciplinary team is extremely valuable and should be part of the standard operating procedure (SOP) for planning any meeting. If a person spends a quarter of a million euros or dollars of the company's money on a meeting and takes 200 individuals out of their professional work for three days, this should be standard procedure. In most cases, meeting owners who initiate a meeting only do one meeting a year. They certainly are not professionals when it comes to investigating and analysing the objectives. Assistance from a method enabling them to do so will be useful and appreciated. Besides the standard single major objective such as "launching a product", a meeting owner will also have the feeling that there is a need for, let's say, interactivity. If someone in his environment tells him about a company that has a voting system, that's usually where it will end. Interactivity, however, is much more complicated and has many more facets than first assumed. There are all kinds and levels of interactivity and in many cases what happens, even with a voting system, is reactivity or activity and not interactivity. Perhaps the real need for this conference is collaboration, or team building, or departmental cross pollination… It takes some thorough thinking and a long checklist to get that ball rolling and to really understand the needs and potential of any conference.

The simplified model of the Meeting Objectives Matrix®:

	List all objectives for the meeting	List how to measure and desired scores
Learning objectives		
Networking objectives		
Motivational objectives		

The holistic approach

One of the key needs for the meeting and conference industry is to approach the content side in an holistic way. Have we forgotten anything? Did we look at everything and do we know all potential objectives for our meetings? Do we really understand all the reasons why we are organising this meeting? Are we focusing our attention and resources on the most important objectives? In most meetings these key questions are either not addressed or, in the best cases, only partially so.

When investing in a new production line or a new warehouse every corporation will have complete and detailed plans and a detailed Standard Operating Procedure. A lot of time is spent by a lot of people in analysing the objectives and designing such an investment. Not so with a meeting, even though the meeting may cost as much as a new warehouse.
Should we not address meeting objectives in the same way?

When identifying the meeting content, usually the meeting owner is on his own. In some cases he or she will be assisted by marketing people or a communication agency, yet most communication agencies or marketing departments have no staff specialised in meetings. If we ask them how many collaboration systems for meetings they know of or what the five levels for measuring ROI are we will probably be met with silence. In order to approach meeting content and analyse meeting objectives, there is a need for specialised people with a comprehensive knowledge. Today there is nobody I know who meets that need.

usually the meeting owner is on his own

Is Mary Boone a Meeting Architect?

Mary Boone tells me she has been a practising Meeting Architect for more than seven years and, looking at her CV, I would be reluctant to dispute her claim. While she has referred to herself variously as a meeting designer and a meeting strategist, her background and the work that she does fits solidly into my definition of Meeting Architect.

Boone's formal education is in the field of organisational communication which is different from a traditional marketing communication background. The field of organisational communication is dedicated to improving communication within and across organisational boundaries. Her studies in communication were focused on a full range of social sciences: psychology, sociology, anthropology, social psychology, HR, training and organisational behaviour. Her Master's thesis focused on effective behaviours of meeting facilitators in electronic meetings.

After leaving graduate school, Boone worked in IT for 20 years helping people apply collaborative technologies effectively to communication challenges. Her book, "Leadership and Computer" was considered one of the first in the field of knowledge management. And the book she co-authored with Dean Meyer, "The Information Edge", was one of the first to apply decision science to the measurement of the "intangible" benefits of IT systems.
She is also a professional meeting facilitator who has facilitated meetings ranging from three to 3000 people for more than 20 years.
More recently, her work in the area of leadership and communication has taken her into the cognitive sciences. An article, co-authored with David Snowden, for the November 2007 Harvard Business Review, was entitled "A Leader's Framework for Decisionmaking". In this, she talks about large meetings as an essential leadership tool for managing complexity.
She is currently teaching a course in organisational behaviour for Northeastern University's MBA programme.

Boone began applying this multi-disciplinary background to the meetings industry in 2001 when she was asked by a friend who owned a meeting production company to help him with a pitch he was working on for a client. Based on her background in organisational communication, she developed her own methodology for setting objectives, assembling tools and approaches, and measuring the benefits of meetings.
When she subsequently tried to engage with the industry on a larger scale, she encountered many of the problems I've mentioned in this book. She was focused on the content side of meetings and it took a long time for her to find the right people to understand her approach.
The prime opportunity finally presented itself in the form of the PEC-NA meeting in Houston in 2008. Barb Taylor Carpender helped introduce Mary to the people in MPI who were responsible for this meeting and she gave a luncheon lecture that talked about interactivity in meetings. She also designed the Conversation Cafes that took place there.

CONCLUSION

Meeting Content – meeting objectives

Meeting content is much more than the content of the presentations. An holistic approach is required for educational objectives, networking objectives and motivational objectives. Each of those three areas is so complicated and there are so many possibilities that an SOP for analysing the needs of a meeting is essential. The Meeting Objective Matrix® is the start of such a procedure. Meeting organisers who spend significant resources should utilise such a procedure to analyse meeting content before allocating resources. Professional help will be necessary because the meeting owner has other priorities and will not have the necessary skills or experience. Such a professional can be a specialised consultant separate from a meeting planner. As the meeting planner specialises in the creation of the environment or the hospitality side of meetings (the shell) the Meeting Architect concentrates on all the Learning, Networking and Motivational objectives of the meeting (the substance).

6. Meeting Objectives Support

Once we understand that meeting content is all about the Learning objectives, Networking objectives and Motivational objectives for participants, we can start to develop the substance of meetings. Knowing those objectives is the crucial first step. After understanding the “why” of organising this meeting, we must now address the question:

“What can we do to support these objectives?”

How do we design and execute the meeting with all the right ingredients such as ideas, people, tools and services that can help us drive the meeting objectives? Turning meeting objectives into meeting design is what this chapter is about.

Definition

Meeting support, short for meeting content support, is everything that can be done at meetings to support the Learning, Networking and Motivational goals. These support activities can be conceptual, human, creative, technical or technological tools or services that are deployed before, during or after the meeting. Meeting support does not include the hospitality aspects of a meeting but does involve the realisation that these are of utmost importance and have a fundamental motivational impact. Collaboration with the meeting planner on overlapping aspects is a must.

Meeting support focuses on execution and offers the meeting owner or Meeting Architect as much support (tools and services) as possible to reach the objectives. In a metaphor involving the construction industry, meeting support is the construction itself, the construction company. A meeting support manager would be the construction site manager.

Meeting Support Tools

3T model

Definition of Tool:

A meeting support tool is anything we can apply or use to support and improve the Learning, Networking and Motivational objectives at meetings. There must be more than a thousand different tools and to ensure we look in all directions we have defined this CHATTY classification for meeting support tools:

- Conceptual
- Human
- Artistic (Creative)
- Technical
- Technological

Conceptual tools are all about the concept, the meeting formats, meeting room layout, and methods such as Open Space, Lego Serious Play, Petcha Kutcha, etc.

Human tools are people such as actors, facilitation, etc.

Artistic or creative tools are tools like, theme, design, video production, creative opening show, etc.

Technical tools are tangible tools which are not computer-related – items such as AV, set and staging, flipcharts, pen and paper, signage, Lego, etc.

Technological tools are all tools that are computer-based – web applications, cybercafé, collaboration systems, networking technology, etc.

Obsessed with technology?

About seven years ago the industry started to pick up on technology and realise its value. Today we see technology appear in all magazines and trade shows. Most of it is about using technology to replace the paper or spreadsheet processes for meeting logistics management – the use of software and the internet for venue booking, event management, registration, etc. These all represent progress and create efficiencies, and the industry is now starting to look beyond the scope of hospitality technology.

don't forget the good old flipchart

The technology that can be used for improving Learning, Networking and Motivation is hardly discussed. This is the part of technology that can improve the results of the meeting based on the meeting objectives. It is therefore the kind of technology that really matters to the meeting's or conference's reason for being. Technology such as electronic networking tools, tabletop groupware, online brainstorming and the like is our focus in this book.

technology is just an enabler

In addition, technology is just an enabler. It is like a new fabric – if you don't have the skilled designer and craftsmen it is just a fabric. Looking at a beautiful fabric can be enjoyable while nothing much happens, but in the hands of the right people it can become a beautiful dress. Creating applications is crucial and the companies that do this are mostly young and small companies. Mercurius RFID is a company that creates applications using RFID technology. They put RFID (technology) tags in a badge (tool) and then write software so the picture of a participant walking into a room automatically appears on a screen to stimulate networking (the application).

If we focus on technology, we may forget the good old equipment like flipcharts, and pen and paper. An open mind for technology and all the other tools (see CHATTY) is what we need – not one or the other but an holistic approach.

Time

After Terrains and Tools the third T-word is Time.

In meeting support, Time addresses what we can do before, during and after a meeting to support or drive the objectives in Learning, Networking and Motivation. How do we get people thinking about the meeting's content weeks before the conference? Can we make them contribute or select speakers or even influence the meeting format or session timings? Most meetings work with a selected audience of specialists. To the meeting organiser it is therefore probably important to capture as much of their attention as possible for as long as possible and in as many ways as possible, including the periods before and after the meeting.

What can we do to prolong the lifecycle of a meeting? Can we get some of the participants to form a community? Can we stimulate networking after the meeting? What can we send them after the meeting as a souvenir with content? And looking at ROI, what can we do to move the learning on to application?

A few examples:

A CD sent to the participants with all the presentations is Educational (Terrain) based on Technology (Tool) after the Conference (Time).

An anonymous online brainstorm to define various topics or changes for the meeting is Educational (Terrain) using Technology / the internet (Tool) before the Conference (Time).

Speed dating is a meeting format for Networking (Terrain) using a Creative Concept (Tool) during the Meeting (Time).

The only thing this 3T model does is provide a framework for thinking about content for meeting planning teams (see Meeting Support Matrix® on p. 86).

Get the basics right

On the one side we have a technology fixation, while on the other a large number of meetings are still facing challenges in getting the basics right. Many meetings are caught in the AV trap. These meetings have a minimal spending culture on AV. They book sound and an LCD projector for the meeting venue. A technician sets it up the night before and that's it. Cheaper than that you can not go. Furthermore, without proper support, rather than aid the meeting it will in many cases get in the way of good presentations, add stress to already nervous speakers and irritate participants. Not being able to understand a speaker, disturbing sounds, technical issues when speakers change and not being able to see the speaker or read the slides are obviously not acceptable. They do, however, occur at a number of meetings. All of these basic things should be right. Anyone participating in such a meeting should protest or get up, leave and ask for a refund.

the AV trap

It is like getting cold coffee, melted ice-cream, or a half-hour wait between starter and the main dish at lunch: no-one accepts that in a five-star hotel. Yet it seems almost normal that in the same venue it is at least partially accepted that AV will cause problems. It does not have to be like this. Meeting planners should be as demanding on AV quality as they are on dinner quality and service.

With more than one speaker and without a technician there is probably going to be an issue. Some planners conclude that AV is unreliable and complicated and therefore will not try anything innovative. They reason: "If even such a simple set of equipment causes problems, it would be mad to go for more complicated stuff." This is the AV trap and these meetings never seem to move beyond the very basic.

To get out of that trap takes the right approach and the appropriate resources. A good technician is certainly part of that. Getting the basics right, preferably with long term suppliers, will create a stable and safe environment in which meetings will start to experiment with speciality tools. This is when meetings start to become what they should be: the pristine and most intense moment in a year for the Learning, Networking and Motivation of groups or communities. There is a trend towards an audience which, at home and at work, has all the tools for the most intense experiences: High Definition TV, surround sound, always online, mood lights, etc. This upcoming generation, born with mobile phones and laptops, will be less and less tolerant of such basic technical flaws and meetings which don't get the basics right will lose participants. The Digital Natives as they are called will need lots of innovative, creative and speciality tools to stay interested in meetings...

Meeting Support Matrix®

The Meeting Support Matrix® is a one-page document with a 3x5 table. It helps teams which organise meetings to design meeting support. Which tools or concepts or techniques can we use to support the meeting objectives that were defined based on the Meeting Content Matrix®? The vertical axis of the Meeting Support Matrix® shows action terrains: Learning, Networking and Motivation. The horizontal axis shows the Tools, thus creating a 15-cell matrix. (The before, during and after (BDA) can be added to the vertical axis to create a 45-cell matrix.)
In the nine resulting cells the meeting design team notes down all possible ideas and tools they could possibly deploy to support the meeting's key objectives. If the most important objectives are networking related, these three cells should be full of ideas in the before, during and after cells.
This is the starting phase in designing the meeting and assists structured thinking.

List all tools that can impact the objectives:

		Conceptual	Human	Artistic	Technical	Technological
Learning	B D A					
Networking	B D A					
Motivation	B D A					

The Meeting Support Matrix shows 15 cells to be used as a note pad at meeting design brainstorms

Meeting support tools

When using the word tools, many will think 'gadgets'. There certainly are gadget-like items available but tools in meeting support are much more than simply gadgets or technology. Tools can be simple or very complex. Some tools were made for daily use and are applied to meetings; other tools were specially designed for meetings while some were especially made for just one meeting. Some tools we can hold in our hands while others are intangible. Some are easy to use and some require technical assistance. Yet others require specialists such as facilitators. Some are very exciting and create a big wow effect; others are very plain but can still score a lasting effect. Some tools are conceptual, some impact the meeting format, and some change the room layout. Some require a long preparation time; others have a quick and easy benefit. Some need artistic or creative input, others are technically challenging.

Let me give some examples of the different types of tools we are talking about.

Simple or complex tools

Simple tools are pen and paper, flipcharts and post-it notes. A more complex tool is the online archiving of presentations with sound, video and slides. This requires AV, production and IT specialists.

Daily use tools or purpose-made tools

Music was not composed for meetings, but some songs can support a certain message or create a desired atmosphere. A purpose-made opening video for a meeting can be used just the once and at that meeting only. It is made to measure for one single meeting.

Tools with or without assistance

An LCD projector in a small meeting is easy to use, but for a widescreen presentation with three or four projectors technical assistance is a must. One wired microphone is fine, but whenever multiple wireless microphones are required, a technician to operate the equipment is a must.

Tools with a high or low wow factor

A simple testimonial from a blind teacher who teaches blind children to work with a computer can also have a lasting impact on many participants – a low wow effect. A big opening show with themed video productions, a VIP speaker, a great act, pyrotechnics and the like generates a major wow moment.

a wide screen presentation for some extra wow

Strategic or operational tools

Concepts such Crowd Sourcing meetings come with a theme which, in this example, is based on the book *"Wisdom of Crowds"* (Surowiecky, 2004). These implement one or more ways of harvesting the wisdom of the crowd. *"The Learning Meeting"* (Alsborg and Ravn, 2007) influences first the meeting format by shortening presentations and creating more time for reflection, discussion and interaction among participants. Other concepts such as *"Open Space Technology"* (Harrison, 1997) are held in an unorthodox room layout with circles of chairs. One I participated in was at the MPI WEC in 2006 where about 20 chairs per circle were used. Lisa Heft has presented Open Space several times with MPI and makes it clear that choosing Open Space is a strategic choice for a meeting's direction. At an operational level, round tables are the consequence.

The Café Conversations we experienced at MPI's Houston,TX, Conference in 2008 are a concept designed by Mary Boone. Café Conversations contain various elements similar to Open Space. This demonstrates the trend towards strategically different meeting concepts allowing for deep participant involvement.

Long or short preparation tools

Delivering a DVD with recorded presentations and the closing video to all participants during a closing dinner takes a great deal of preparation. A quick effect can be added at the last minute by deciding on a closing video – a well-edited three-minute report with music.

Arty or techy tools

Adding some drama to a conference by hiring an actor to make a fake speech can be very powerful, but the right actor and the perfect script is needed. Using software to match people and organising one-on-one meetings, or dinners with table topics, takes technology and IT support.

As described above, there are many kinds of tools and many ways of looking at tools with the aim of supporting specific objectives in meetings. As of 2007 there was no centralised complete list or "bible" of meeting support tools. There must be hundreds of tools which have a small and local market or are waiting to be discovered by the meeting industry. The Meeting Support Institute is building a knowledge base of many of those tools.

Specialty tools

I am convinced that few people are aware of even 10% of the tools available today. Simply reading through the latest edition of 'Vision', the Future Lab's twice-yearly magazine on technology in (school) education, proved to be an eye-opener for me – about seven times.

I have probably missed several categories of tools, but it should be clear that a meeting which uses only a microphone and PowerPoint is not exploiting the real potential for its Learning, Networking or Motivation objectives.

If we wish to do a good job on the content side – managing the meeting's objectives – it also is clear that we need a lot of time to Investigate, select, analyse and prepare the meeting support tools and services. But how do we integrate these into a complete and flawless concept that really drives the objectives? We are not talking about a few hours but about days, and the Meeting Architect would probably provide some guidance in that process.

Meet Different was the theme of MPI's conference in Houston 2008. This conference demonstrated in many ways that MPI, the industry's largest association, was taking bold steps toward the learning side of meetings. Different alternative formats, Open Space, co-creation, Wiki workshops and other new projects were showcased. Many more sessions than usual were dedicated to education, facilitation, games and learning, meeting 2.0, etc. One of the most daring sessions involved nTag's Rick Borovoy who allowed himself to be scored continually throughout his presentation and accepted our judgement. When this dropped below 50% he ended the topic he was addressing. Rick not only spoke about Meetings 2.0, he enabled us to experience it!

The Future of Meetings: Learning, Technology & Connections: This well-attended session with Bruce M. MacMillan CA and Elliott Masie invited all participants to co-create the future of our industry, a very interactive workshop that also addressed the content side of meetings.

More about MPI on www.mpiweb.org

Meeting Support Company

In 1999 Abbit Meeting Support became the world's first company to use the words 'meeting support' in its name, and then put the term on the map through presentations, publishing, advertising and trade show presence. It made meeting support its single mission as a company. Many companies perform some part of meeting support but do not have a focus on meetings. A lot of companies, for example, provide all the necessary AV for a meeting but not the specialty services for Education, Networking and Motivation. Some will also work for exhibitions or concerts, which does not give them the right focus for meetings.
Some companies have a meeting focus but service only a part of the meeting support scope. They specialise, for example, in meeting presentations but do not provide all of the other services. A meeting support specialist will offer every service or tool that can be used for supporting the content side of meetings.

This is a new business model and a reasonably successful one too, but the enormous task of including all tools and services creates a steep learning curve and plenty of investment.

From AV company to meeting support company

An AV company which makes the decision to become a meeting support company has a long path of innovation, training, hiring and change ahead of it. It takes some nerve to take the step, but the change can provide great value. Obviously the main income for such a company will remain in AV. With an increased emphasis on all other services for meetings, however, the AV equipment part may become smaller and the dependence on it less. This may help to cope with some of the new competition in the AV branch, where the cheap and portable LCD projector has become a no-brainer.

A meeting support company must be of a certain size to be able to manage all support aspects and be home to all the different skills needed for the full range of these. IT certainly plays a major role in meeting support for offices, registration areas, cybercafés and presentations. Then there are the aesthetics and construction skills for designs and signage, set building and staging, multimedia skills for producing DVDs, CD-Roms, online presentations, etc. These and many more skills are much more diverse than the sound technician, the lighting technician and the projection technician of today's general AV company. Many services need to be provided in-house.

The vast and ever increasing number of tools and concepts plus the endless variation of applications in a niche market, makes a meeting support company a valuable concept. It provides a multidisciplinary team of co-ordinated individuals who, working together in briefings and brainstorming sessions, can come up with the best solution for any meeting objective.

AV companies may be obvious candidates to become meeting support companies, but that does not exclude others from joining in. An IT company could become one, for example, or it is possible to imagine a meeting support agency evolving from a production company with all the knowledge but working with subcontractors for the execution.

In-house AV

AV people who understood the meetings industry saw good business in organising in-house AV for hotels. Some of these companies have become large in the US. It is understandable that a venue wishes to be able to offer this service and in many cases that is a good solution. The venue does not invest but gets an implant from a large AV company. If the venue receives a commission, everyone is happy. However... I believe a meeting or conference deserves better than this kind of service. Meetings are far too important to leave them to ever-changing in-house teams. A meeting owner must look for continuity and build on a trusting relationship with a travelling partner. In-house technicians are not really interested – every day a new client means a tedious factory production-line situation with no relationship, no connection and, as a result, less engagement.

- exclusive AV clause
- no long-term, no traveling relationship
- meeting remains at basic AV level
- meeting is less productive
- meeting indsutry is vulnerable

how exclusivity clauses hurt the industry

Venues which have exclusivity for AV services in their contracts obviously don't help the industry or themselves. It is not helping if meeting owners are prohibited by a venue from continuing a long-standing relationship with a vendor. Such meetings never grow up from a basic AV level, making the event less productive and the industry more vulnerable.

The venues also damage themselves because the professional meeting organisers (the good clients) with an ongoing relationship with their suppliers will not break that safe and stable situation but rather choose another venue. A 2004 survey from MPI Belgium and a student's research from 2005 show that a significant portion of meeting planners avoid working with venues which have such exclusivity clauses. It also showed that local exclusive suppliers tend to be more expensive.

Meeting Support technician

Just as we all expect a sufficient number of waiters to ensure that a seated lunch runs well, we need sufficient technicians to get the basics right, a few more to create a professional meeting and a few on top of that to create perfect presentation support or full-scale meeting support. We're not talking about a technician who sets things up the night before, but technicians who also operate equipment, intervene if problems arise and support the speaker in whatever he or she wishes to accomplish.

Technicians and AV companies must be aware of the fact that meeting planners are irritated when they see technicians doing nothing, playing on their laptops or reading a book or even a newspaper. And rightly so. Technicians are paid to work and that's what they should do. Technicians should be taking pictures of the meeting, recording the sessions or doing whatever adds value to the meeting. There are many opportunities to fill that gap. Technicians who do not wish to perform multiple tasks and learn new skills are not in the right industry. They even threaten their own jobs if meeting planners conclude they are not doing anything and therefore will not be booked for the following event.

A good meeting technician is a meeting specialist. Not a rock 'n roll sound guy who also does the occasional conference to fill his calendar.

A meeting technician is multifunctional and will cover sound, projection, PowerPoint and much more. This is especially important for smaller (50 to

100) or low- budget meetings, or in meetings with parallel sessions in break-out rooms. A multifunctional meeting support technician can be the sound specialist in the plenary room and cover all technical aspects in one of the break-out rooms. This is cost efficient and also ensures that the technician work for his money rather than spending most of the time doing nothing during presentations.

A meeting technician from a non English-speaking background should also speak fluent English. This is an absolute must for international meetings or meetings with international speakers.

A meeting technician has experience with meetings and understands and eases the stress of speakers rather than causing it.

The value of good, trained and specialised meeting technicians is obvious when you see how happy meeting planners become when they work with a motivated and skilled meeting technician.

Maintaining stability in meeting technicians by travelling with them, results in good things – consistency, stability and predictability in the service level of that person, the opportunity to build rapport and create reliability, and the security of having someone you know rolling in big flight cases with who-knows-what inside them. Finally, the stability of cost can be an issue for budget prediction.

Definition of meeting support technician

A meeting support technician is a technician with a clear focus on meetings. He or she is a multi-lingual (with good English as a minimum) technician who performs multiple tasks: combined sound, lighting, ICT, voting... The meeting technician understands the basic processes at meetings including stress handling with speakers.

If you have a lot of tools, services and technicians at a larger or more complicated meeting, and you want it all planned ahead, you may consider working with a team leader we call the Meeting Support Manager.

Meeting Support Manager

BEFORE

The Meeting Support Manager is an individual who is the one contact person and acts as the liaison between the meeting organiser and the meeting support company. This person plans and executes all meeting support services for a meeting. The Meeting Support Manager helps the meeting owner in planning and leading the execution of all solutions for any meeting objective. In the design phase he or she will provide ideas for tactics as well as operations to support the strategy.

The Meeting Support Manager is also the person who will plan the entire technical and creative package for the conference. A Meeting Support Manager needs a few months (and sometimes gets only a few weeks) before the conference to plan everything, including floor plans, shipping, crew, briefings, call sheets, etc. The phase before the conference or meeting is crucial. This is when choices are made and decisions are taken which determine the meeting's success and its level of ROI. Spending enough time with Meeting Support and remaining dedicated to the objectives will not necessarily cost a lot but will innovate the meeting in a way that increases value and saves money. The Meeting Support Manager books equipment and people, and makes scripts, scenarios and cue lists.

dedicated to the objectives

DURING

On site, the Meeting Support Manager makes everything happen. He works with a team of technicians and the equipment that was ordered. The Meeting Support Manager's core objective on site is to get the best out of the available people and equipment in the most efficient way possible. He or she joins the pre-conference meetings, presents at a speaker briefing, makes sure technicians are on time and, during the meeting, gives the cues, takes the role of stage manager and is a problem solver.

The Meeting Support Manager remains calm when everyone else is nervous. He translates client remarks such as "what is that strange sound" into "check wireless 6 and equalise it around the 600hz". After the conference he ensures the room is cleared of confidential information, that everything is packed and loaded for shipping and that recordings are copied for back-up, etc.

AFTER

The Meeting Support Manager can start planning for the next conference immediately after the previous one. He or she becomes part of the meeting team and helps in the change and improvement process. In the construction metaphor, he is the construction site manager. The Meeting Support Manager will not, or only partly, be involved in the hospitality side of the meeting.

He or she needs to be a mature person with a specific skills set. A background in production or AV is good, and planning and communication skills, leadership and creativity are some of the other characteristics.

Definition of Meeting Support Manager

The Meeting Support Manager is the project manager for meeting support. He or she is part of the meeting organising team and focuses on the combined production, AV, ICT and other content-oriented services. The Meeting Support Manager plans and leads the tools and people for meeting support. On site, the Meeting Support Manager maximises the impact of available people and tools. He or she is the one contact person for all content-related services.

Identify objectives	Designing	Executing	Assess results
Strategic	Tactical	Operational	
Meeting Owner	Meeting Support Manager	Meeting Support Manager	
Meeting Objectives Matrix®	Meeting Support Matrix®	Meeting support	
6 months before	6 to 2 months before	1 month before, during, & the months following	The day after until the next meeting

Focus on meetings

A Meeting Support Manager must have a clear focus on meetings. As with the meeting support company, a Meeting Support Manager needs to know all the specific services and tools for meetings. The focus on meetings is crucial: Dealing with speakers, knowing what educational efforts are to be set in motion, the specific AV support and the like, makes the value of a Meeting Support Manager somewhat different from a production professional who "also" does meetings but mostly does theatre, events, concerts and parties.

The focus on meetings will generate hundreds of areas where specific knowledge is needed. Take speaker timing – this is not really necessary for parties, but a good automatic countdown system for speakers can be crucial in conferences. When installed on a PC, the natural reflex of a Meeting Support Manager is to wire that same PC up as a back-up for the PowerPoint PC.

Meeting Support Knowledge

Technical and practical knowledge is the next crucial factor. A Meeting Support Manager does not need to know how to equalise an AKG 4000 wireless head-worn microphone with a Yamaha O1V, but it helps. He has to know that a good sound technician is able to do that and makes sure it is done before the meeting starts. A Meeting Support Manager needs to know the different types of microphones and maybe even the brands of these. Besides his comprehensive AV knowledge, a good Meeting Support Manager also knows a great deal about production, staging, presentation technology and specialty services like voting, collaboration technology, networking technology, ICT, etc. This package of knowledge is massive and requires continuous updating. At Abbit Meeting Support a regular Techno Demo is organised to share the latest innovations. Many specialised technical workshops are also organised. Being on the mailing list of the Meeting Support Institute (see p. 99) and going to trade shows can help in the quest to stay up-to-date.

growing complexity

Long-term collaboration

Working with a different team every year, a conference organiser will have to put in a lot of effort in order to get the basics right. The quality will rise and fall and there is no chance of introducing valuable new tools or services. Long-term collaboration with a Meeting Support Manager and preferably his or her team makes the process of executing the operational side of meetings consistent, easy, predictable and financially stable.

If a conference or meeting starts to test and use innovative tools and services it becomes crucial to have a trusting relationship with the meeting support manager. The growing complexity and increased use of technology make stability and continuity a must. A long-term relationship with a Meeting Support Manager not only delivers stability in execution but the Meeting Support Manager can also take part in an improvement process that allows for true innovation.

When is a Meeting Support Manager used?

Realisation of what working with a Meeting Support Manager means makes it difficult to imagine how a professional job can be done without such a person. For some smaller projects involving one room with a simple AV set-up and two technicians, it probably is not necessary to have one. If, however, we take 50 sales managers out of the office for two days or spend more than €100,000 on a meeting it may be a good idea to get a Meeting Support Manager on board.

The traditional reflex of asking the meeting planner to book AV is fine for small and simple meetings. The meeting planner would then usually book local or in-house AV. But people need real meeting support when they become nervous about the next conference's AV and technology, knowing that last year a lot of things went wrong. For those who are still struggling to get the basics right, it's time for an improvement process.

Some meeting planners may resist this kind of thinking because it enters their professional space and may siphon off some of their responsibilities. It will soon be clear that meeting planners, like the whole industry, can only benefit from this approach.

Clients who understand the complexity of meeting support often involve the Meeting Support Manager early on. In the planning process a client will have the Meeting Support Manager join site inspections. The selection of a venue is increasingly based on the meeting support manager's input. A Meeting Support Manager is interested in room height, obstructive chandeliers or pillars, the loading dock, backstage facilities, rigging points and power. These factors are increasingly weighed up in making venue selection decisions.

The Meeting Support Institute

Starting as an AV company and slowly growing into a meeting support company, then defining Meeting Support itself was a long process of some 15 years. At that time I felt somewhat isolated in the meetings industry even though I had chosen it as my industry. It is probably the warmth of the meeting industry and the many friendships with its members that kept me going. I started to realise that something should change in order to give my ideas the chance to grow – the market was not focused on what we were doing and it took us lots of explaining and convincing to make new customers see the potential. I started to look for a bigger, more global approach. I knew there were other companies in the same position in an industry that did not realise what to us seemed so obvious. I could see that we were too small to make a difference on our own so started to think about an association for those companies. The idea of the Meeting Support Institute was born. In 2003, when doing my CMM with MPI, I was ready to put the plan on paper. For the CMM (Certification in Meeting Management) which focuses on strategic thinking, we needed to do a business plan. Mine was entitled: "The Meeting Support Institute". I got my CMM in 2004, began experimenting in 2005 and officially opened for membership in 2006. Our two founding sponsors are IMEX and Starwood.

Goals, Mission

The meeting industry is losing innovative products to the marketing industry. The EIBTM award winner is one (see case p. 42), and another innovative company says the same: "We can't seem to find decision-making clients in this industry." They did a full demo of their product, a powerful collaboration and co-learning technology (groupware), at a large meeting planner conference and soon afterwards shifted their commercial focus towards the marketing industry, away from the meeting industry.

Every year, more potentially ground breaking and innovative companies do the same. They enter the meeting industry, fail to find a connection and leave. This is because meeting planners are mostly focused on hospitality and leave the content side to the meeting owner. The question for the meeting industry is if and how we wish to stop that process of losing innovative young companies. The challenge is that 'meeting owner' is not a profession and probably never will be. Most meeting owners only become meeting owners for a few weeks a year.

There is no association of meeting owners. They may be members of a marketing association, a CEO club or the like but not of an association of meeting owners. They would not have the time or motivation to spend a day at a course for meeting owners because they organise only one meeting or conference a year. This shows there is no single place for these innovative companies to go. If they focus on CEOs they will need to fight for attention. If they focus on the marketing industry, they probably have the best chance but are still are competing with media, internet and other marketing tools that demand the marketing manager's attention. The key objective for the Meeting Support Institute is to create a welcoming environment for those innovators in the meeting industry.

Expanding limited knowledge and limited choice

The fact is that the meeting owner knows of only a limited number of tools and services. The people who assist the meeting owner are marketing or communication professionals and their knowledge of meeting support tools is also limited. If they accidentally discover a collaboration system, this may be experienced as the ultimate innovation and contracted to impress participants. The meeting may be better off with another system, but if they have no opportunity to find these different suppliers, comparison is not an option. The choice and information are limited. Finding such a company is therefore a lucky shot. I believe that the Meeting Support Institute should make the connection between support tools and meeting owners/planners. The goals of the Meeting Support Institute are diverse. It has members who all provide a service, knowledge or value, and there is the target audience of meeting planners and meeting owners.

The first level of membership is companies with a product or service which impacts Learning, Networking or Motivation at a meeting. Then there are the intermediates such as production companies or PCOs which use meeting support products for their clients. Following that group are the consultants and individuals such as meeting designers, creative meeting directors, facilitators, ROI specialists, trainers, etc.

In addition to promoting commercial products and services, there is also an academic angle. There is useful knowledge in the Learning Lab Denmark, the Future Lab UK, the HR faculty of St Ambrose University in Davenport, Iowa, and hundreds more such organisations. The professors, scientists and academics form all kinds of departments at universities which can help us with data and knowledge that can be used in meeting design and meeting processes.

On the receiving end we have meeting planners and meeting owners. They are the end users of meeting support and Meeting Architecture services. The second receiving group involves the universities and other educational institutions which may wish to start a course in meeting support management or Meeting Architecture.

Between these there are connectors such as the media, trade shows, meeting association conferences and other "transmitters" to pass on the information. The MSI supports magazines in publishing articles, chapters or supplements.

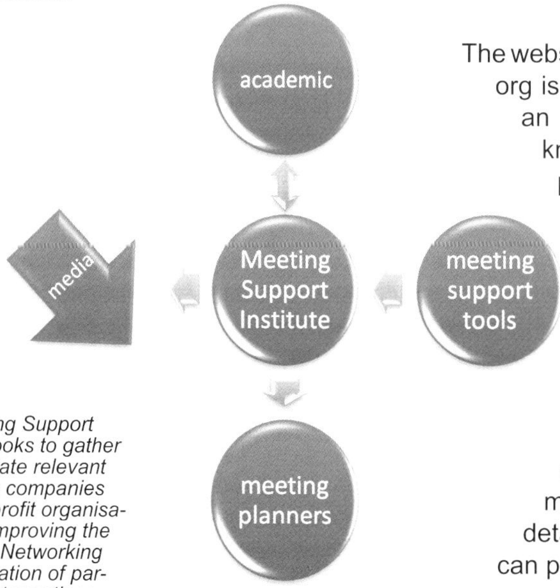

the Meeting Support Institute looks to gather and translate relevant input from companies and non-profit organisations for improving the Learning, Networking and Motivation of participants at meetings.

The website www.meetingsupport.org is open to anyone and has an increasingly significant knowledge base of books, people, websites, articles and more. These are all relevant to anyone who is working on the content side of meetings. It is helpful to improve the Learning, Networking and Motivational objectives for participants at your meetings. The membership list provides details of companies which can provide services or tools.

The activities organised by the Meeting Support Institute are aimed at educating and promoting the use of meeting support techniques and tools that improve the results of meetings. The Institute organises group stands at trade shows, presentations and other educational occasions. There is a regular newsletter while educational activities are organised to enable members to learn and meet other meeting professionals who have a strong interest in meeting content.

The holistic approach

Meeting support is the holistic approach to supporting meeting objectives. It aims at providing and applying all existing knowledge, techniques, methods, formats, tools and services that have an impact on meeting content or meeting objectives. It is not just technology. Neither is meeting support only about AV or facilitation. It is about all of the above and more.

Meeting Content Support is not just about supporting the presented content but about all Learning, Networking and Motivational aspects of meetings.

One of the challenges in our industry is the diverse but non-integrated offer of suppliers. But each tool or service is only a small part of the range of things we can do. The meeting owner or meeting planner needs professionals who can inform him or her about all or at least a large number of options for each meeting objective.

What currently occurs is random and unsystematic. With comprehensive resources and an holistic approach, alternatives can be investigated. Selecting one from many options should result in more efficient spending and optimal meeting results. As complex, challenging and diverse as the objectives of meetings can be, so too should meeting support be diverse, flexible and versatile.

This takes us on to the next chapter where we introduce the concept of Meeting Architecture and how a Meeting Architect could be the interface for all of that.

CONCLUSION meeting support

Meeting support is both a concept and a business model. It approaches the services at meetings from the meeting objectives perspective: the Learning, Networking and Motivational goals. Meeting support consists of all tools and services: Conceptual, Human, Artistic, Technical and TechnologY, (CHATTY). It requires a total focus on meetings and an holistic approach so that all available tools can be considered for driving a meeting's objectives in the most efficient way. The meeting support technician, the meeting support manager, the meeting support company are all to be considered for long-term relationships so the required improvement process can kick in. The Meeting Support Institute is a resource for finding innovative services and up to date knowledge

7. The Meeting Architect

Meeting Architecture as a new profession – that is what this book is about. Going from AV services to meeting support to Meeting Architecture was and still is a long and exciting trip. Being involved in meeting content is probably one of the more strategic positions in any company: it is helping to translate the corporate mission into good delivery through its most powerful communication tools: meetings, conferences, events.

Definition of Meeting Architect

A Meeting Architect is an individual who focuses on the potential meeting objectives, the meeting formats and designs, and the conceptual and practical building blocks for constructing a meeting aimed at better learning, networking and motivation in the participant population. He or she also knows how to measure the meeting results up to level 5 ROI.

Meeting Architects as I define them here do not exist yet. The ultimate goal is formal education, certification and a Master's degree in Meeting Architecture. We have a long way to go but it will be a rewarding journey.

A new profession is about to be born

The content side of meetings as discussed in previous chapters is of such great complexity that it is safe to say we need a new profession. If we take the business of meetings and conferences seriously, we need to make this happen. The arguments are obvious and the most powerful is the complexity of scientific and technical knowledge. The world of the meeting planner is a complex one and the world of the Meeting Architect is at least as complicated. It certainly uses knowledge and needs skills which are complementary to those a meeting planner needs. This chapter will look at several sciences and industries the Meeting Architect will need to learn from and keep learning from on top of knowledge about meeting support tools and services.

Other consultants

There is a wide range of consultants who are all close to or part of Meeting Architecture. Depending on where we are, what we do and who we know, we may be working with one of those categories.

Let me give you some examples of the kind of consultants we have today.

Marketing and communication consultant

If we are marketing professionals in a corporate environment we may know a marketing or communication agency or two which could help with the next meeting. They would approach a meeting from a communication angle and focus on the key messages, design printed material, branding and PowerPoint. They would probably not get into the networking potential, the sociology and many other potentials of the meeting.

PCO

As association meeting owners, we may work with a PCO (Professional Conference Organiser) which spends the majority of its time on logistics and hospitality. It may also get into the content side for making an abstract book or poster session, but most will remain on the surface and will not (yet) move into, or be allowed into, the analysing of meeting objectives.

Specialty service company

If we are lucky enough to know a collaboration technology company or an electronic meeting support company, we may get some good analysing of objectives on the learner side and some good technology support on site, perhaps even facilitation. The results will show a large amount of rich information.

Facilitator

Then there is the facilitator, the speaker trainer and even the drama specialist who can all bring valuable improvements to meetings.

A product or format consultant

We have the Lego Serious Play (www.seriousplay.com) certified consultants and the Open Space consultants (www.openspaceworld.com) as well as many others we haven't heard of yet.

Meeting designer

Some very fortunate meeting owners know someone who calls himself a meeting designer; a rare breed. He or she may be a creative or even artistic person who focuses on the objectives and handles the theming, the meeting format and maybe some of the processes which take place at meetings.

All of the above companies and consultants bring some degree of serious value to the meeting table. None of the above, however, has the holistic approach a meeting owner needs. They all approach meeting content from their specialised and limited angles and use only a particular section of the potential services and tools. This is what will differentiate the Meeting Architect from the specialist above: he or she will know the above professions, individuals and companies, and will call on them according to the defined meeting objectives after thorough analysis.
Should a meeting owner happen to know one or two of the above suppliers, he or she can become quite excited about working with them. What he or she does not realise, however, is the range of other options available. The meeting owner needs a Meeting Architect. The Meeting Architect will be a catalogue, an interface, translating the needs of a meeting owner into design elements and building blocks for that meeting.

Building that missing profession

There is a great deal of work to be done to build the knowledge base for Meeting Architecture. We need to combine all existing science, professions, knowledge and tools into one big knowledge base. Based on that, books need to be written, courses designed and curricula for university degrees assembled. I am convinced that graduating with a Master's degree in Meeting Architecture will take two, maybe three years. And it will need a continuing education programme to enable people to stay up-to-date with the latest scientific and technological developments.

I do not believe that Meeting Architects will take over from the consultants mentioned above. There are two things that may happen: these specialists will decide that they will remain specialists and the Meeting Architect population will take them on board for clients who need them. The other path is that a specialist, let's say the facilitator, decides to become a Meeting Architect. Studying, reading and taking courses will develop and widen the knowledge of such an individual to the point where he or she would become a (certified) Meeting Architect.

A meeting support manager is not a Meeting Architect: we need to keep progressing in the direction of Meeting Architecture. Some current meeting support managers may become Meeting Architects if they wish and take on the study involved. But it will not be a five-day course and a certificate that makes a good Meeting Architect. Nor will it be a Master's degree in Meeting Architecture. It will take years of practice as a meeting planner, meeting support account manager or maybe meeting support manager

it will take years of practice

CASE:
A recent and ideal example is the following case. Abbit was involved early on with the account executive, the meeting support manager and myself in the role of Meeting Architect.

We approached the project with what we call MAP, the Meeting Architecture Process. We had a few long meetings where first we inspired, secondly investigated objectives and then designed the meeting before going into the execution phase. During the first meeting we introduced the concepts, the methodology and the matrix. At the second meeting the real work started. Six people spent a total of three hours or more analysing the goals and objectives.

As in an ideal world, the client had lined up the meeting owner, the Meeting Planner and the Meeting Content Manager – a unique situation with the triangular team (see illustration on p. 132) which shows that companies really are interested when given the option. We used the Meeting Content Matrix®, so looked at the Learning, Networking and Motivational goals. Then we used the Meeting Support Matrix® and listed all we could to drive those objectives forward before, during and after the meeting. In those meetings alone we spent some 70 man-hours (including the client and Abbit) before we started to produce even a PowerPoint template. This is how it should happen, especially with meetings of a certain budget. That it doesn't always happen is due to three reasons:

- One: You don't miss what you don't know: "It was never done before."
- Two: If I understand the need for such a process there still may be "no time".
- Three: If I can do it and want it: "There is no-one to help us with that process."

The Meeting Architect will be an answer to all these objections.

Building a house without an architect

If you decide to build a house, you will contract an architect without hesitation. Designing a house is performed in detail with the help of an architect because a house costs money and a great many specialists and building blocks require co-ordination. You would not even think of building the smallest house without an architect because it is obviously a professional's job. As a painter or sculptor, you would not think of building a house without an architect. As a handyman, a great leader, an entrepreneur or a procurement person, you would still need to build that house with the help of an architect. So it should be with meetings.

Although a meeting often costs as much as one or more villas, meeting owners still build that meeting themselves – without a Meeting Architect. If a corporate manager built a warehouse without an architect, that manager would be held accountable. When it comes to meetings, however, managers can get away with sub-optimal results. Large and important events such as meetings should not remain deprived of what we consider evident when building a house. The only thing that stops us from doing so is that we don't have Meeting Architects; even if you wanted to book one, a Meeting Architect does not exist yet.

What's in a name...

Meeting Architect: If we start using the term it will become meaningful.

I believe the term Meeting Architect says it all. Everyone can relate to it and it has no bad connotations. Sure, the title is of less importance as long as we agree that there is an opportunity for a new profession and we understand what the responsibility will be.

Below are a several relevant titles used in this book:

	A.k.a.	Description (also see definitions in this book)	Construction / Building metaphor
Meeting Owner	Meeting sponsor	Initiates the meeting, knows the subject, the objectives and target audience	The landlord
Meeting Planner	Meeting hospitality manager	Specialist in travel, logistics and hospitality for meetings	Finding and preparing the right piece of land and preparing it for construction. Making the house habitable, providing a road, electricity, water, cables, etc.
Meeting Architect	Meeting content manager	Specialist in identifying objectives, designing meetings around objectives, executing and steering the meeting towards its objectives, assessing results	The architect
Meeting Support Manager		Specialist in the execution, technical side of the meeting, managing AV, ICT and much more	The construction site manager
Meeting Support Technician		Specialist technician who is multi-functional, multi-lingual and can handle speaker stress, even ease it	Bricklayer, plumber, electrician
Meeting Specialty Services		All other specialised professionals such as facilitators, moderators, designers, creative directors, producers, communication or human processes specialists, specialty tool providers, etc.	Suppliers of building blocks: bricks, pipes, cables, switches, wood, etc.

To create Meeting Architecture, we need to develop a vocabulary and a methodology. The mere act of establishing the title Meeting Architect may result in a paradigm shift in the meeting world.

As long as there is no established title for anyone who may be doing this work, the profession will not exist. No-one will ask for something that does not exist. Just as the meeting planner had to fight for years (and still is) to be recognised, so too will the Meeting Architect have to be patient. However, if the Meeting Architect is as defined in this book and knows what is sketched out in the curriculum, he will soon be recognised and talking to the right people.

The word architect in Meeting Architect rings more than a bell. Almost any adult has a good understanding about what an architect does and can translate that to meetings. Most people respect an architect as a specialist and a professional who is essential to construction design and quality.

Depending on the ambition of the Meeting Architect and the size of a project, he or she could end up in different positions in team structures.

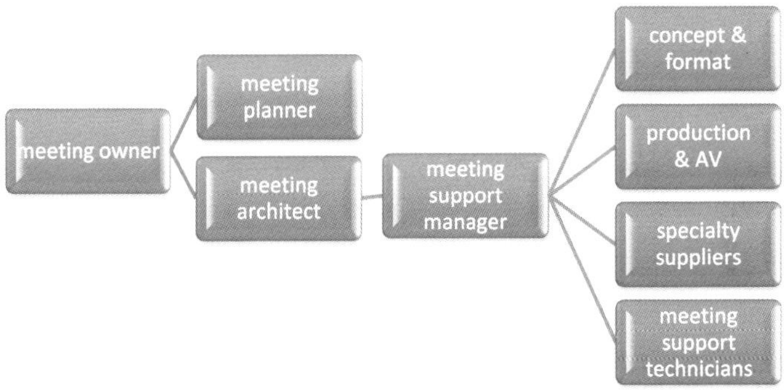

In a simple organisational chart the Meeting Architect's position could look like this

In a more sophisticated situation or larger organisation the Meeting Architect could lead a department and projects. A senior meeting planner could grow into that position and the organisational chart could look like this:

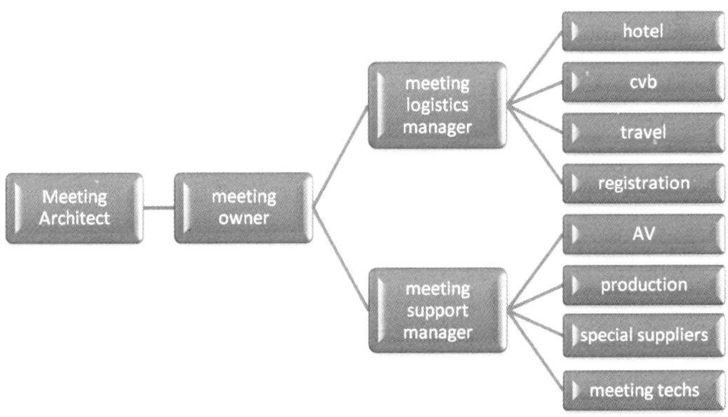

This senior Meeting Architect is part of the strategic marketing team .

Many more organisational structures can and will exist. Just as no organisational chart of any company looks the same as the next one, so will the Meeting Architect fill many different positions and find himself at many different levels of responsibility. The level of sophistication and strategic impact of the profession as I envision it is such that it has the true potential of receiving that long-awaited seat at the table for the meetings industry.

The four phases of a meeting's annual lifecycle

In the lifecycle of meetings there are four crucial phases, similar to those an architect who is creating a house works through.

An architect will talk to the family (his client) first and see who they are, what they do for a living and as hobbies, what they say they need, how much land they have, what the budget may look like, etc. The architect gathers information, analyses the needs and identifies the objectives. The better the architect, the more time that will be spent on this phase. The second phase is the design phase. The architect draws sketches and plans. These plans are discussed, adapted, weighed against the budget and finally result in a model. In the same design phase, colours, doors, textures, tiles, wood, wallpaper, fixtures, taps, switches, etc. are presented and selected. The budget is finalised.

The third phase is the construction, the execution, phase. The building begins, the technicians build and the architect leads the work with a construction site manager, based on his plans and monitoring the budget. The final fourth phase is the measuring: Assessing the final result. Are the walls and windows as planned? Is the plumbing and paintwork up to spec, is the building as expected?

Exactly the same four phases take place in the lifecycle of a meeting and could be managed by the Meeting Architect. The difference in this case is that the meeting client orders a new "house" every year so an improvement process can be established and results will improve year on year.

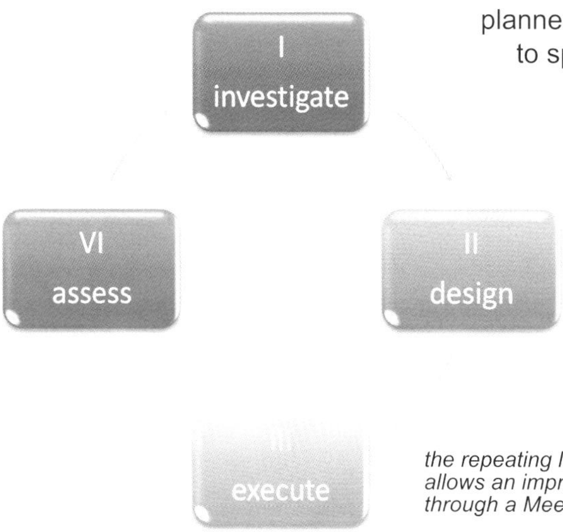

the repeating life cycle of annual meetings allows an improvement process and innovation through a Meeting Architect

The management process for the Meeting Architect is based on repeated investigation, design, execution and assessment.

IDEA

IDEA is an acronym for the four phases:
Identification of objectives
Designing the meeting based on those objectives
Executing the meeting
Assessing the results

Phase I: Identify Objectives

The first time a meeting is planned or the first time a Meeting Architect becomes involved, analysis is the most important phase. On p. 56 we address the "Why" question and come up with a range of potential objectives. Many meeting owners, however, have a difficult time addressing that question thoroughly and answering in a structured and complete fashion. It takes a great deal of time, a thousand questions and a lot of thinking to come up with a complete and ranked list of all objectives that need to be addressed for the meeting. The meeting owner, in his mind, has a pretty good idea of what needs to be done, but usually will not see all that could be accomplished. A meeting can influence and impact so many things that a detailed checklist as part of a methodology is a must.

identifying key objectives

When a meeting owner starts with one or two major objectives, the result of a thorough analysis may show five or more key objectives and even a dozen sub-objectives. Each of those sub-objectives may result in several action points, suggested in the design phase and implemented in the execution.

Most meeting owners have a hard time coming up with a good briefing and the Meeting Architect therefore needs to get his or her information by asking questions. Having the right people around the table is a prerequisite. In the hierarchy of organisations, an AV or production company currently sits down with a meeting planner and tries to come up with a plan. That plan then needs to be approved by the meeting owner, let's say a product manager, who was not present at the meetings. One level up in the hierarchy, the VP marketing controls the budget and has a final say based on what he or she hears from someone who heard from someone how things could be done. Many good ideas and innovations never reach the design phase because the right people were not present when they were discussed or presented. A Meeting Architect's first task is to analyse the hierarchy and penetrate deep into the decision-making chain. The very fact that "the architect is coming" may attract attention from the higher level decision-makers. The situation is similar to that of the future owner of a house who hasn't much to say to the bulldozer operator but becomes involved and excited when the architect arrives. The title alone may be what we have missed in trying to get to the right people. If one aims at improving the results of meetings, a direct line of contact with all involved to the highest level (the budget owner) is a must.

The Meeting Architect could also play a role in all meetings of one organisation and be part of the strategic marketing team. In the case of a large corporation, a department of Meeting Architecture or a team of Meeting Architects could be lead by a senior Meeting Architect.

The identification phase is the strategic phase. This is where the meeting is linked to corporate strategy and the strategy of the meeting is developed. The Meeting Objectives Matrix® or similar should be used in order to obtain a detailed and structured overview of the meeting objectives and their importance. In order to give this phase sufficient time, identification of objectives should start six months before the meeting.

Phase II: Design

Once we establish a list of objectives we can start thinking of designing the meeting. Today, many creative producers or directors and meeting designers must start off with an incomplete briefing and therefore a limited understanding of what the meeting is all about. They must then dive right into the design process. Good work in Phase One is crucial.

Form must always follow function, not the other way around. Therefore design (form) should start only when the objectives (function) are clearly identified and defined. A creative person might be better off staying out of the process until the meeting team has a complete and precise briefing on all the objectives. Some meeting owners are simply looking for a big wow effect and just take the most exciting idea, not really connecting it to the

> it is like carpet bombing
> versus precision bombing

objectives. The wow factor in a meeting can be a hazard to its ROI. The wow in the opening show is like the catering – an easy success if you spend enough. It is "easy" to impress a crowd by throwing $300,000 into a big show with a famous singer, half the Cirque du Soleil and a famous author as keynote speaker.

There should be some wow in every good meeting. Many opening sessions I have seen, however, have a huge wow factor and then almost nothing is done for the break-out sessions or any of the Learning, Networking and alternative Motivational objectives. In the design phase we manage this balance between what we defined as key objectives and where we spend the budget. That requires standard operating procedures and obviously is a lot more work for the meeting owner than selecting the best-looking offer for a spectacular opening session and spending all the money there. It needs a lot of designing to ensure all the objectives are supported. It takes a lot more knowledge and work from the organising team and Meeting Architect to build precise and targeted wows in every little area of importance. It is like carpet bombing versus precision bombing. Carpet bombing is much more spectacular but not necessarily as (cost) effective as precision bombing based on intelligence.

Obviously if we have a meeting of 5,000 participants with "celebration" high on our list of key objectives and a budget of two million dollars, it may be right to spend $300,000 on the opening and closing night shows. Not so if we defined education or networking as the number one key objective and have a total budget of only $500,000.

Designing a meeting is about timing, format, guidance, tools, techniques, consultancy, methodology, technology and the like: all based on the objectives. It is about finding the right building blocks to execute the designed meeting or finding the right ingredients for the chosen menu.

Some of these ingredients should be tested unless we know the chef's reputation. In the meeting design phase, the Meeting Architect will present or demonstrate a number of tools to choose from – like an architect working on a hotel who will

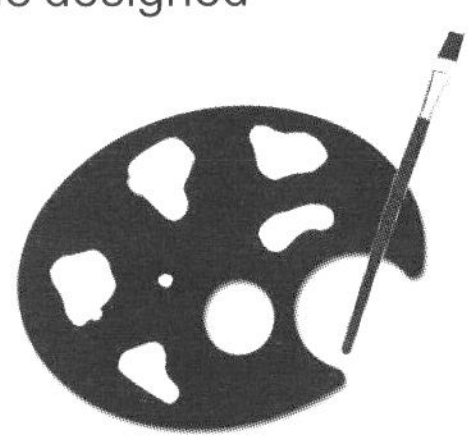

select and present different mood boards with the fabrics, wood samples, furniture designs and paint colours for each space in the building. Some techniques are new and some technology untested. Some risks may be taken but a step-by-step incremental adaptation of the meeting design is to be advised in most cases. Some meetings may require radical change to save them from extinction but an improvement process of analysing and re-analysing, designing and redesigning, is a great thing for any meeting.

A good Meeting Architect will constantly be looking for new formats, new techniques, new technology and new knowledge to add to his tool box.

The design phase is the tactical phase where we develop the tactics and select the operational elements to support the strategy. In the design phase, the meeting team may grow. In addition to the meeting owner, Meeting Architect and meeting planner, the meeting support manager and the creative director could join the team. They would represent the execution side and bring creative ideas and tools to the table.

In the design phase we should use the Meeting Support Matrix® and its methodology or SOP. The completed Meeting Support Matrix® should be on the table and a final meeting design should include a signed Meeting Support Matrix®. A final list of activities and tools to be deployed has to be in place together with a budget that is close to final. Just as the plans of a house are signed by the architect, owner and a construction company, so too could the Meeting Support Matrix® be signed by the parties involved.

Together with the Meeting Objective Matrix®, this forms the plan. Now we need to execute it and build that meeting. Ideally this phase should occur four months prior to the meeting and be finalised two months prior to the meeting.

Phase III: Execute

The building starts a few months or, in worst case scenarios, a few weeks before the meeting. The building process is based on the design (Phase II) which was based on the objectives defined during the identification of objectives (Phase I). If analysis and design takes 75 man-hours, the actual building, including activities before and after the meeting itself, can easily take up to five times more. This is when creative designers and IT technicians start to prepare, planners book equipment and crew, floor plans are getting technical details, facilitators and speakers' briefings take place, images are selected, videos edited, sets designed, voting questions prepared, and specialty suppliers booked and briefed for their educational, networking or motivational input, etc.

Online activities and communities are activated, a Wiki or blog is set up, presentations are tested, texts are written. The Meeting Architect is a very busy person and could be assisted by a meeting support manager and his team. This is the operational phase where things move from the drawing board into action, from theory into practice. This is the moment when the meeting support manager gets really active. Videos are produced, a team is assembled, scripts are written. The execution starts before and reaches its climax during the meeting with all technology, facilitation, recording, etc.

The completed (and signed) Meeting Support Matrix® is used to check on how all meeting support tools selected in the design phase are deployed. The output is all the activities that are executed (III) based on the design (II) and supporting or driving the objectives as identified in the identifying phase (I).

Meeting support activity for the meeting participants starts as soon as design has reached maturity. It starts before the meeting with teasers, theme introduction, online brainstorming on the topics, SMS (text messages) activities, etc. This can be developed a month or two before the meeting and start building up to the meeting at about the same time. Speaker briefings with a PowerPoint template and advice on the meeting format should arrive at the speakers' desk at least a month before, and the opening video also needs a few weeks for development. The most intense moment obviously comes during the meeting, and meeting support continues after the meeting with online presentations, follow-up mailings, answering unaddressed questions, photo albums and other reminders up to a month or two after the meeting.

Phase VI: Assessing results and reporting

After Phases I, II and III (identifying designing and executing the meeting) it is time for assessing or measuring the results and seeing if we have reached our set objectives.

Reporting may be the task of an ROI specialist or could equally be the Meeting Architect's job. How did the meeting go? Did it go as planned, did everything work? How did participants react? What did they learn? Are they using what they learned and what is the impact of that change? And finally, looking at cost, what is the financial return on investment? Just as an architect looks at the house he helped build and checks on the results, so too the Meeting Architect has a responsibility in the final result of the meeting. If the objectives were a, b and c, how did we score on these objectives?

going full circle

It is obvious that deciding on the way this is measured can best be part of the designing phase. If the survey questions are built together with the design of the meeting, a clear and logical connection is embedded. It becomes more difficult when an ROI specialist becomes involved after the meeting. He or she must also be totally immersed in the objectives before starting to develop the measuring tools. The measuring can start during the meeting by testing participants before and after sessions. This not only measures but also increases recollection and so improves learning (as shown by a 2005 study in psychology).

The connection with the next meeting (continuation and tying as the C and T in PERFECT) and the fine-tuning of its objectives is best done by one and the same person. This continuity is of utmost importance. Even if the meeting owner is replaced, the Meeting Architect can bring consistency and improvement to the table. The participants remain largely the same and the new meeting owner should move forward from the previous year's meeting rather then start all over again or do a lesser job. The ROI report and other feedback from the previous meeting is the best foundation for the next meeting and so the Meeting Architect goes full circle by doing the measuring too.

The Meeting Architect, in some cases assisted by an ROI specialist, reports to the meeting owner.

We can use existing ROI methodology. Many books have been published on this subject, including "Proving The Value of Meetings & Events" (Jack Phillips, Ph.D., Monica Myhill and James B. McDonough, 2006).

General feedback, suggestions for improvement and an intermediate ROI report should be presented between one and two months after the meeting. Depending on the level of ROI the meeting owner wants to measure (levels one to five) an ROI report should be final a few months or even weeks before the next meeting starts.

This table lists the relevant elements in each of those IDEA phases

IDEA Phase	Identify objectives	Design	Execute	Assess results
Level	Strategic	Tactical	Operational	Reporting
Who	Meeting Owner Meeting Architect	Meeting Owner Procurement Meeting Architect Meeting Planner Meeting Support Manager Creative Producer ROI Specialist	Meeting Owner Meeting Support Manager Meeting Support Technicians	Meeting Architect Meeting Owner ROI Specialist
Tools	Meeting Content Matrix® methodology	Meeting Support Matrix® methodology	Meeting support suppliers, technology, creative and technical tools (AV, etc.)	ROI methodology
Output	A list of objectives and a strategy for the meeting	A format, a schedule, a meeting identity (theme, logo, slogan, theme song) Floor plans, set design. A list of tools and services A budget	Professional flow and execution of all designed elements before, during and after. Participants walk away with the maximum of learning, networking and motivation as set out	Knowledge about the results of the meeting and suggestions for improvement
When	6 months before	6 to 2 months before	2 months before, mostly during and a few months after. As soon as design is ready	The day after until the next meeting
Supplier	Meeting Architect	Meeting Architect Meeting support company	Meeting Architect Meeting support company, specialty suppliers	Meeting Architect

Let's get some science involved

The part of the meeting and conference industry with the bigger budgets currently has a strong link to production. A great deal of attention is given to the wow effect. Meeting owners get a kick above and beyond the kick their audience gets. It is a moment of fame and a moment when one feels like a Hollywood film director. But is this objective-based?

The Meeting Architect will support such a large production only if it fits the objectives and does not divert resources from other essential objectives. The Meeting Architect aims to use the budget in a balanced way based on those objectives. The kick of big and loud productions is literally a adrenaline kick, the same kind of rush people had when attacked by a lion in 10,000 BC. This old adrenaline rush was designed to make us run or fight. In big and spectacular productions it makes us feel as if we're on a high.
This little bit of neurology brings us to the scientific area a Meeting Architect will need to study. Much scientific evidence (old and new) can be applied to meetings in order to improve results on all objectives, whether educational, networking or motivational. The challenge again lies in building a knowledge base that is relevant and applicable. Filtering the right material from a range of scientific areas will be a task for many individuals from outside the industry. Once that is done the knowledge needs to be translated for meetings and integrated in the curriculum for the degree of Meeting Architecture.

Neurology obviously has a lot to teach us about how our audience learns or forgets – the memory, the effect of testing, eating, alcohol, coffee and sleeping, the amount of knowledge an average participant can absorb, the different senses, etc. New portable technology in the shape of a cap or a scarf allows the scanning of brains of individuals in action. Can we imagine research being done on how many participants drift away during a presentation and are thinking about something completely different? Can we imagine a roomful of participants connected to a brain meter which shows how awake an audience is during a particular presentation? How long can a presentation keep the brain in an Alfa state rather than the Beta sleep state?

how awake an audience is

Psychology may have even more to offer particularly in the terrain of Motivation. What is the effect of a specific activity on the participants? When do we lose the participants' engagement to learn? Concepts such as priming, subliminal messages, chunking, mnemonics, social loafing and Lewin's freeze phases are all applicable to meetings. Books like *"The Wisdom of Crowds" (James Surowiecki, Abacus 2005)* cite many psychology research projects as does the stimulus-response relationship from behavioural psychology as part of *"Objectives to Outcomes"* (Glen C. Ramsborg, 1995).

Sociology and social psychology clearly impact Networking and help us understand group dynamics such as group talk. Networking for introverts is an interesting topic on which research has been done.

Biology has dozens of areas that connect to meetings – things like food and sleep for example. The influence of the gender of teachers on the results of pupils has been demonstrated. Boys score lower grades with female teachers and girls score lower grades with male teachers. What is the impact of that effect on meetings?

Then there is a professor of networking at a university, in the US, who specialises in corporate networking. Is that becoming a science too? We must ask this professor to spend some of her time and thinking on meetings and conferences. If she could write a chapter or a book, or have a student produce a thesis on networking at conferences, that would be a major stepping stone. Producing valuable books on that topic should not be a problem. Most books on networking speak to the individual and give advice on how to be more successful in networking at events or on the web. What the Meeting Architect needs, however, is information on how his design can influence, improve and drive networking at meetings and conferences.

more research to be done

Some good research has been done and is being done but much more needs to be done. Inviting these and more different scientific fields into our industry will generate a wealth of knowledge for improving on what we do today. Bringing it all together in the Meeting Architect's mind would be an amazing step forward. All the knowledge is there for the taking. Someone has to bring it all together so people can learn it. Is this a mission for academics and universities?

Let's get other industries involved

Industries such as marketing, the facilitation world and the training community will also be sources of knowledge and inspiration. Specific elements of many industries should be harnessed based on their applicability at meetings. After adaptation to the meeting industry practice and vocabulary this needs to be bundled together in a book and become part of the Meeting Architect's knowledge base. Let's have a look at a few of those industries.

Marketing and communication

I assume that some communication agencies must be tempted to put the title of Meeting Architect on their business cards. I would agree that they are great candidates for such a title and that what they do today is certainly part of it. Communication clearly is a crucial element in the scope of the Meeting Architect – the communication industry and its knowledge base is part of what any Meeting Architect should know.
In many companies, the marketing department is the home of the meeting and conference planning department.
The marketing industry or education may also be interested in taking ownership of Meeting Architecture as a profession.
Large marketing companies will probably hire future Meeting Architects for their events department.

HR

HR is an industry as well, and again has its own education, trade shows, magazines, associations, etc. This industry, like the marketing industry, is very much involved in meetings. HR also knows a lot about training and that closely relates to what happens at meetings and conferences. HR people get a lot of psychology and sociology during their education so in many ways are immersed in parts of what a Meeting Architect must know.

HR and marketing are not only industries; they are also departments in companies and as such, in some cases, HR people are meeting owners. In that sense they are, like the marketing industry, a double stakeholder – as an industry they are a provider of knowledge, and as a client they're a user of Meeting Architecture.

AV and production industry

AV and production companies are a similar industry. Many producers of events and many AV specialists are a potential source of knowledge for the Meeting Architect. The Meeting Architect needs to understand the difference between a handheld and lavaliere microphone. He or she needs to know when to use what kind of loudspeakers The Meeting Architect must be able to estimate the cost of a certain package of lighting and know when to go for back projection or LED screens. The AV industry probably has a few hundred services that should be part of the Meeting Architect's knowledge. Many production managers would be potential Meeting Architects, and production companies are certainly also interested in hiring future Meeting Architects.

Training industry

Looking at the education side of meetings, the training industry is certainly a source of inspiration for the Meeting Architect. This is a large industry with its own magazines, trade shows, courses (train the trainer) and books. The ROI methodology in the meeting industry is derived from the training industry and there surely are interesting links towards the analysing, designing and execution of meetings and conferences. If the measuring (ROI) methodology can be translated from training to meetings and conferences, these other phases in the lifecycle of meetings are at least worth looking at.

(Adult) education industry

The education industry is probably larger than any other. Schools and universities are factories of education and the schooling system takes the largest part of our government's budget. Adult education is an industry in its own write and again the knowledge that resides there has great value for our industry. Then there are institutions like universities of education; educational institutes which work on education. A project run by one such institutions, the Learning Lab Denmark, is "The Learning Meeting" which has conducted a great deal of research and produced a book named *"Learning Meetings and Conferences in Practice".* This is a perfect example of real meeting-focused output from an existing industry, in this case the education industry.

Facilitation world

Professional facilitators, I think, are very much under-estimated and in many cases not even considered. I would suggest to corporate boards that any meeting spending above €200,000 must appoint a professional facilitator. The processes among people at meetings are so crucial that good facilitation can prevent meetings from failing in certain critical areas. Facilitation is really a core competency in Meeting Architecture. Some facilitators may become Meeting Architects and most Meeting Architects would probably hire facilitators for their larger meetings. A facilitator is to a meeting what the web is to a Wiki: an enabler of processes among groups of people. The facilitation industry is an industry too, although not of the size of marketing or education. Facilitators have an association named AIF, the International Association of Facilitators, with information on their website:

www.iaf-world.org and www.iaf-Methods.org

There are a number of books, degree programmes – e.g. a degree in international communication and facilitation – CPF Certification for Professional Facilitators and a conference run by ASTD (American Society on Training and Development). Meeting Architects could certainly register to attend such conferences.

Virtual meetings industry

There is a part of the AV equipment manufacturing industry that is all about equipment for video conferencing and other types of virtual office meetings. This industry is clearly rich in technology and innovation: text to speech and speech to text, recording of sessions and making them available for others in a rich-media and searchable manner, etc.

Real meetings should welcome virtual meeting technology and become in many cases hybrid meetings where a real meeting is supplemented with remote presentations and remote participation. If a VIP speaker can not be present, why not have a remote presence? Why not create remote participation for a few VIP panellists or even participants who can't make it, even if only for one or two sessions.

Technology is evolving. The Meeting Architect should be aware of all the technological building blocks available in this area and thus be able to make use of them when a meeting's objectives demand it.

Drama

Even if some people may not necessarily consider drama or theatre and actors as an industry, it still forms part of the Meeting Architect's toolbox. Using an actor to deliver a message or using a virtual character on the screen during the opening session are yet more means of influencing the Learning and Motivational processes at meetings. In the Learning Lab Denmark, a doctorate on Drama in Meetings is on its way.

If we assume that actors and facilitators are on the same playing field, they are still very different building blocks to be used by a Meeting Architect whenever the meeting design needs them. Actors, and how to use them in meetings and conferences, again represents more material to be studied and absorbed by the Meeting Architect.

Books to read

There are a number of books out there which clearly fit into the world of Meeting Architecture. The bibliography on p. 154 is certainly not complete, but these books are of the sort that I would consider recommended reading for Meeting Architects.

Some of these books are an easy read and others are large text books in their particular fields, such as the "IAF handbook of group facilitation".

If we take a closer look at the bibliography of *"Objectives to outcomes: your contract with the learner"* (Glen C. Ramsborg, 1995) we'll see that this lists more than 70 (!) books on adult education, evaluation, behavioural psychology, etc. There are clearly more than sufficient books to choose from. Creating a curriculum should not be a challenge because of a lack of books, but because there are so many to choose from. Even if you doubt that there will be as much choice in the areas of Networking and Motivation composing a sound curriculum for Meeting Architects is clearly doable.

Many books, textbooks or study books still need to be written. Many of those books will be "selections from" psychology, sociology, communication, etc.:

existing elements relevant to meetings which are brought together and result in a new book focused on meetings and conferences.
Some other books on meeting-focused topics such as 'Motivation at meetings' need to be written as do practical workbooks on, for example, analysing meeting content and its methodology. Several ideas can be seen in Books to be written on page 155.
The total list can clearly be massive and the reading of those on it is an option for a multiple-year course.

Magazines to sign up for

General psychology magazine
A magazine on sociology
Cognitive science
Meeting Support Institute newsletter
Vision from the future lab
etc.

Associations to join

When Meeting Architects hit the market, there is going to be a need for an association which caters to their specific needs. In fact, there are so many fields in which they should join an association that it would become a fulltime job just attending all the conferences. Their own community will have to form their own associations and organise own conferences.

Membership of MPI, PCMA or ICCA would certainly be an option.

Continuing education

The Meeting Architect will visit different trade shows, register for different conferences and read different magazines than those a meeting planner does today. Some meetings trade shows, conferences and magazines will include some of the popular Meeting Architecture topics for their population of meeting planners in order to keep their readers up to date. Some Meeting Architects will also connect to these media but will also read psychology and register for one of the technology in education conferences.

Like a doctor, a lawyer and an architect, so too must a Meeting Architect follow continuing education in order to stay informed.
What a meeting owner wants to hear from a Meeting Architect is the latest and most up-to-date innovations for improving the results at the next meeting. It is not simply about large and high resolution screens for spectacular shows, but also creative concepts for greater involvement, the latest in smart technology for better networking, or scientific research which alters the timing of the programme.

Sony Anycast: innovation with big impact on camera use in meetings

This would represent a continuous effort for both the providers of education and the Meeting Architects. Conferences, courses, trade shows, etc. will all grow as the population of Meeting Architects grows.

The architect styles

Meeting Architects will have different backgrounds. Some meeting planners will grow into Meeting Architecture, some facilitators or producers will become Meeting Architects, etc. Some will start at 18 and graduate aged 20 or 22, some will get a certificate at the age of 44. In the same way that there are different individuals coming in, the Meeting Architects will be different too.

Every Meeting Architect will have his or her preferences and put his or her own accent or emphasis on different aspects. For some Meeting Architects, the emphasis will be mostly on communication; others will have a more artistic approach and underline creativity and originality of ideas. Some will create a stylish look and feel and behave more like the designer of an experience. Others will be engineering types and technology will get more attention...

every architect will have their own style with their own preferences and accents

In the same way that houses have walls and a roof, meetings have a number of standard necessities that any Meeting Architect has to include and manage. Therefore a Meeting Architect must be universal, multi-functional – an engineer on the one side, and creative and adding his or her accents on the other. A good Meeting Architect should know all the options, all the building blocks and be willing and able to use them depending on the core objectives of a meeting.

The Meeting Architect's professional choices

As with architects in the construction world, there will be different career paths for Meeting Architects to choose from. Some will be one-man companies and others will be working in a team or a group. Some agencies like event agencies, independent meeting planners or PCOs may hire Meeting Architects as they graduate. A third option would be Meeting Architects working in a corporation as part of the meeting or conference department. A last example is a Meeting Architect who works in an audiovisual or meeting support company. All of these formats have advantages and limitations. Depending on the needs, the type of meeting or personal preference a meeting owner could decide to work with one or another.

The meeting planner and the Meeting Architect

Whenever I speak to meeting planners about this idea of Meeting Architecture and the Meeting Architect as a new profession, I get different reactions. Some like it, some don't. Some say "that is exactly what we need" and some are reluctant or hesitant. Recently I spoke to a full-time meeting planner who does 20 meetings a year and she asked: "How many meetings can I do if I need to do all that stuff?" The answer is "fewer than today". Let's say we find the time to become a Meeting Architect and the time to stay informed – if we want to do a good job in all four phases of the meetings we plan, it would probably take twice the time. I think it would be a challenge to do 10 a year in her case. All depends on the type and size of the meetings, but it is clear that analysing, designing, executing and measuring will be at least the same amount of work as planning and managing all the hospitality and logistics.

But if the meeting planner has more than enough work with logistics, who will do it? The idea of adding a second person just for the Meeting Architecture is for most meeting planners a paradigm shift. Many meeting planners are positive because they will be able to focus on what they like – the tourism and hospitality side of the job. Some seasoned planners see an opportunity – they prefer the meeting content side and would hire someone new for the hospitality and logistics work.

The marriage

In addition to the challenge in time and sheer volume of work, the skills needed for each of these professions are quite different. The hospitality person will be "of a different make" to the Meeting Architect. They will have different and complementary skills. Hospitality is more about the welcoming, warm and patient attitude. Are we all happy and did we lose anyone? It's all about taking good care of people and catering to the individual whims of clients, a passion for travel, accommodation, catering, etc., and leading a group from point A to B. Those extrovert skills are quite different from those of the Meeting Architect who operates in the background, works with learning processes, networking psychology and all kinds of science and technology. This person needs more technical, analytical, statistical and scientific skills. If opposites attract, this could be a good couple.

The reverse case

In January 2007, Dorcy Bowman Rose, an independent meeting planner told me about a "reverse development". For several years Dorcy worked at a large corporation where she was involved in the organisation and execution of meetings. She was responsible for the content, analysing, designing and executing of the educational and marketing side of this company's meetings. She loved her job and when she became independent called herself a meeting planner because she felt her strength was planning meetings. Dorcy owns the internet domain name meetingplanner.com and she soon discovered that she was hired to primarily assist with the logistics and hospitality side of meetings. "It is a challenge to find the kind of work I was looking for and experienced in," she said.

It is clear there is a long way to go and that this will be an evolution that takes 10 or 20 years. No-one's job will change overnight because the words "Meeting Architect" are printed on a business card. It will be a gradual process of learning, experimenting and constant improvement. Although changing the title may have an impact, it will take a lot of advocacy to convince the decision-makers to change policies. A clear signal such as the start of a Master's degree in Meeting Architecture may be essential to that effect.

A divorce?

An industry friend is Robin Lokerman from MCI. When we were talking about the Meeting Support Institute he asked me why I wanted to split the meeting content management away from the hospitality management. I think it is safe to say that it is not about separation but about making it part of the industry: bringing them together. Look at the trade shows, look at the magazines, look at the associations… As long as 98.5% of advertising and trade-show floor space is filled with destinations and venues, there is nothing to be taken away. Once IMEX, EIBTM and other meeting industry shows are 75% venue/destination and 25% meeting content, then it will be part of the industry. Once the magazine advertising is 10% about the content side, it will be part of the industry. Today, meeting content does not really exist as part of the meetings industry. It may be one of the things PCOs and association management companies do to a certain level, but it is not really out there. What the Meeting Support Institute and this book aim at is attracting attention for the content side of meetings, to making it visible.

The goal is to inform, motivate and support development. That becomes clear if we look at the Meeting Support Institute knowledge base. Its objective is to create a resource for anyone working on the content side. We invite people who have some relevant knowledge to come in and maybe focus some of their resources on it.The goal is to create, to co-create. Not separating, but joining. We only create attention by placing it in the spotlight and by avoiding distraction from what is already so evidently established.
Yes, it is right to look on it as a different profession. The Meeting Architect will be a separate profession for the reasons mentioned above. There has to be a separate degree, a subject I will address in the next chapter.

The gender balance

A side effect we could predict is a return of the gender balance. Today, associations such as MPI are 74% female. If the meeting industry welcomed and supported development of the content arena, the diversity in the industry would increase. I believe more men would become part of the industry and the gender balance may be restored somewhat. Although this is not a goal, it may just be an additional benefit since more diversity can only be good.

The holistic approach

The knowledge is dispersed across different industries, scientific disciplines and professions. Some people know a lot about adult education, some about facilitation, some about networking and some about motivation. Some companies are great at producing a highly motivational opening show but have no interest whatsoever in what happens in the educational sessions. Some companies have a voting system and will not easily advise a meeting organiser to use a zero cost, pen and paper solution even if this would be better suited to that specific conference objective. A neutral consultant such as a Meeting Architect would be the best to ensure the right choices are made.
The holistic approach is the only way to go. This will require some people to spend some long and hard studying and training time. There is a lot of material out there, but it needs to be brought together in a structured way. This would enable meeting organisers to find what they need rather than act on the basis that a friend of a friend knows this company with one solution. Currently the Meeting Support Institute makes that effort through a knowledge base on www.meetingsupport.org The ultimate result is a new profession. A person specialising in the content side of meetings would be a full-time and specialised professional called a Meeting Architect. The efforts involved in achieving such an holistic approach will be significant, but the result for the industry will make it worthwhile.

The Meeting Architect embodies the truly holistic approach to meeting content or meeting objective management. A Meeting Architect must study all there is to know about the content side of meetings: about the Learning, the Networking and the Motivational objectives for participants. A Meeting Architect should know all tools that can be applied and be open to the latest trends without forgetting the good old flipchart and all its possible applications. A Meeting Architect is involved from A to Z, from identifying the objectives to measuring results.

A Meeting Architect knows <u>all</u> the potential objectives of meetings and conferences and helps the meeting owner to see objectives he or she did not realise were possible.

A Meeting Architect knows <u>all</u> the building blocks with which a meeting can be constructed and will consider all of them in the design phase. These building blocks can be techniques based on scientific knowledge, formats based on sociological experiments, services like facilitation, technology for networking, etc. All the knowledge that today is fragmented and dispersed must be united in Meeting Architecture.

Meeting Architecture brings it all together in the production phase and may be involved in all actions before, during and after the meeting. The Meeting Architect could be directing the video production or just checking the scenario before production starts.

After the meeting the Meeting Architect will be able to deploy all existing techniques to measure the meeting's effect.

The meeting owner, meeting planner and Meeting Architect

The meeting owner is a professional leader in marketing, sales, product knowledge, etc. He or she could be the CEO, HR manager, or VP Training and Education. The meeting owner will not necessarily be the one who knows all there is to know about meeting content and potential meeting objectives.

The meeting planner we know today is a busy professional specialised in creating good logistics and a perfect environment for a meeting to take place. The skills needed for this are varied, but the main ones I see are good planning skills (organised, deadline, project management, etc.) and a passion for travel and hospitality. The meeting planner needs a fine sense of what a group will need in order to feel comfortable and welcomed. Taking good care of a group is not an easy job, especially when it involves experienced and spoiled professionals. It means working with VIPs on the one hand as well as comforting a participant who is angry about not getting the right meal for his gluten allergy. It means staying calm in all circumstances, even if the waiter speaks only a rare Portuguese dialect and we need that gluten-free meal urgently. A meeting planner has a natural tendency toward the travel, hotels, leisure, entertainment and incentive side of meetings. It takes passion and a warm, welcoming mind-set to build a closing dinner that has a wow effect. Those skills are what I would call heart-oriented skills – friendliness, warmth, spoiling others, an eye for beauty and style, and a welcoming attitude. In one word, hospitality.

different skill sets

The Meeting Architect works on the content side and requires a different skill set. Some meeting planners don't wish to become involved in this because they have too much work or simply prefer the hospitality side.

When confronted with the possibility of a voting system for his meeting, a planner replied: "Please don't go there. If we give those speakers a voting system, they will be asking a lot of questions and I have no time." In this way, the meeting remained stuck at a minimal AV level and did not develop into an advanced and innovative learning event. Many meetings don't reach their full potential because no-one is confronted with new possibilities. As long as no-one asks, there is no need for new solutions and as a result such a meeting uses only a microphone and LCD projector...

Two meeting planners at a trade show were asked if they were involved in the content side of meetings and they replied with a "NO, thank you very much!" There are of course other, perhaps more senior, meeting planners who do get involved in the content side and are even combining both the shell and the substance, the meeting environment and the meeting content. Some like the combination and others would prefer to specialise in one direction.

Meeting content (investigating objectives, designing and executing) requires skills such as teaching, science, analysis, creativity and group dynamics. These people will tend more towards education, communication, writing, business objectives, metaphors, creative, technical and technology.

Ménage à trois?

Although there must be a few people out there with the skills, passion and drive to cover both the hospitality and the content side, I doubt there are many who would really pass the test for both.

The skill sets are very different, staying informed on just one is challenging and working on both will require so much time that physically I believe it just can not be done by one person. I would suggest that meeting departments of large organisations and PCOs or other independent meeting planner agencies start to hire specialised staff and organise for two distinct professions working together in one meeting and events department. Using marketing, HR or communication people who undertake meeting objective management only once a year is not the best solution. The specialised Meeting Architect will in many cases have a background in one of these professions, cognitive science, or psychology but should specialise in or be passionate about meeting content.

Professional development (PD) specialists we see in associations are obviously also candidates to take on board the entire load of meeting objectives. Whereas today they specialise in selecting the right topics and speakers and support them with AV and other practical matters, tomorrow they could also take on board all of the other educational issues as well as the networking and motivational activities.

This holistic approach will also make sure that budgets on the content side are spent in a balanced way – the right amount on the opening show, educational support and networking efforts.

In the next chapter on meeting support we will look into more practical things that could land on the Meeting Architect's desk. For meeting organisers who mean business and want the best results from their investments, it will be clear that a separate professional will have a great deal to work on.

Brain side

Focus on the substance

Investigate design,
execute & assess results
of meeting objectives
in learning,
networking,
motivation

Body side

Focus on the shell

Create appropriate
travel and hospitality.
Manage quality
and safety
for group
and individual
wellbeing

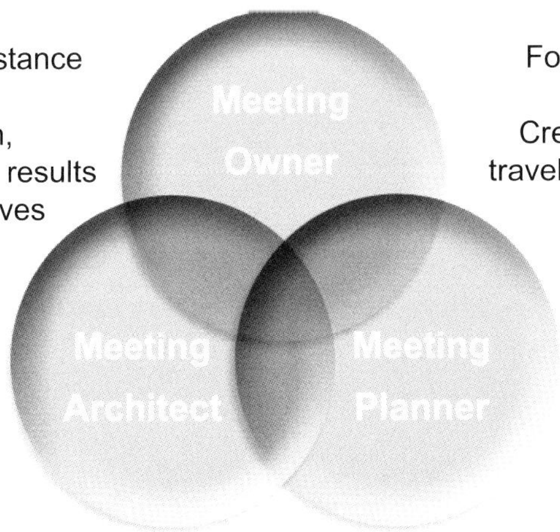

The triangle – one meeting owner supported by two specialists who focus on a specialised domain

Conclusions on Meeting Architecture

Meeting Architecture is a new title and profession that may be a stepping stone for the meeting industry into a new stage of development. When Meeting Architecture becomes an accepted practice and a conventional part of an organisational chart, the meeting industry will move from its current, challenged position to a strategic level. Meeting Architecture may help change the perception of meetings as a cost centre to a strategic lever and a revenue generator.

Today there is no-one who can claim the title Meeting Architect as defined in this book. There is no place we can go to become one, no book or magazine, no resource other than that started in 2006 by the Meeting Support Institute. This represents a great opportunity for the meetings and conferences industry to develop that profession and become the "owner" of it. For magazines, for trade shows, for associations in the meetings industry it creates growth potential, career opportunities, new markets, new resources and revenue.

It will require real and long-term support from the big players in the industry, and assistance from universities and schools that may venture into a new (Master's) degree for Meeting Architecture. Without their support nothing much will happen. It will require a vision above and beyond short-term benefits. It will be about engagement by the industry through giving back and investing in its innovation and progress for the benefit of all.

E-mail comments to the author at maarten.vanneste@abbit.eu

8. A degree in Meeting Architecture

Why?

A two or three year Master's degree in Meeting Architecture may be a long way off but I believe we need to aim for it. There is a place for it, there will be students and the industry will soon start asking for more once the first Meeting Architects hit the streets. It will, in a simple way, drive the industry forward.

Positive influence on the meetings market is one reason to start a degree in Meeting Architecture but another important reason is the complexity and the sheer size of the knowledge base. I believe it is a step forward to add hours to current meeting management curricula but I also believe this will soon lead to a separate curriculum for an additional year and a separate Master's degree. It will simply be too much for one student to study the relevant curriculum for both current meeting management and Meeting Architecture.

Getting other faculties on board

An interesting thing to discover is how easy it may be for some universities to start a degree in Meeting Architecture. Look at the list of all post-graduate degrees at the University of Westminster. I looked at this university because I know Rob Davidson, the Senior Lecturer in Business Travel and Tourism. Professor Davidson is excited about the potential of Meeting Architecture and is one of the academic supporters who are helping to look for ways to get this on track. I was looking for the curriculum of MA Conference Management when I stumbled across the list of post-graduate degrees. Scanning through this list and looking for the Meeting Management course, it all suddenly became clear. The list contained a large number of the ingredients for a course in Meeting Architecture! More than half of those degrees (30 of 57) included some of the knowledge that could or should be part of the curriculum.

Post-graduate degrees at Westminster University, London (2006)

Architecture
Art and Design
Asian, Chinese, Cultural and International Studies
Biosciences
Business and Management
Communication and Creative Industries
Complementary Therapies
Computer Science
Conference Management
Construction and Surveying
Diplomatic Studies
E-Business/Commerce
Electronic Engineering
English Literature
Estate Management
European Studies
Fashion
Film
Finance
General Management
Geography
Health Care Management
Health, Community and Social Care
History
Housing Management
Humanities
Human Resources and Personnel
Information Management and Business
IT
International Relations
Interpreting
Journalism and Mass Communication
Languages
Law
Leadership
Marketing and Marketing Communications
Mathematics
Media
Music
Photography and Imaging science
Planning
Politics
Property
Psychology
Public Health
Social Sciences
Sociology
Technology and Design
Tourism
Translation
Transport Studies and Logistics
Urban Design
Urban Regeneration
Visual Culture

The Curriculum

When we think of an endeavour such as a new profession and a new Master's degree, we obviously get to the point where someone drops the word "curriculum". A curriculum is the set of courses or topics that a school or university would teach for a degree in Meeting Architecture. It took one conversation with Janet Sperstad, CMP, to get that ball rolling. Janet is Lead Instructor in the Meeting and Event Management Program at the Madison Area Technical College. As an MPI member, Janet was chairwoman of the organisation's Professional Development Strategy Group in 06-07 of which I was a member. She put me in contact with Sue Tinnish, a consultant and speaker on meeting-related topics.

Sue Tinnish spontaneously sent me a list of some 300 topics plus a few etceteras. You will probably think of another five or 10. This demonstrates that there are like-minded people – it's good that some are starting to connect. It also shows that such a course will be extensive and will probably take one or maybe even two years full-time to complete.

It is also clear when we look at the lists above and below that they match nearly 100%, even though they come from two sides of the Atlantic. The proposed topics for the degree in Meeting Architecture are almost all part of a course or degree taught at Westminster University. All Professor Davidson has to do is get the right people around the table and start the degree. If everyone can be convinced, it is probably only a matter of finding the right sponsors. There are hundreds of universities and schools worldwide which can carry out this exercise and, with existing staff, faculty and facilities, start a course within a year or so. If two professors from all 30 relevant departments at the Westminster University teach an average of 16 hours per year, we have a new course. It sounds do-able to me, and I look forward to seeing how the process will flow and provide help where possible. Starting a university Master's course is not my cup of tea and it is probably not as simple as I envision it. Many academics and institutions, however, are willing and able to make that happen, and some have already started with initial steps towards a course in Meeting Architecture in 2007.

some

already

started

Outline of Curriculum Elements by Sue Tinnish

1) How People Think and Learn
   a) Brain & Biology (neurobiology)
      i) Right Brain/Left Brain/Whole Brain thinking
      ii) Generational Differences (fMRI studies)
      iii) Gender Differences (fMRI studies)
   b) Learning Models
      (1) Andragogy (Malcolm Knowles)
      (2) Others
      (3) Experiential learning
   c) Principles of Adult Learning
   d) Emotional Components
2) Writing Learner Outcomes
   a) Common vocabulary: Goals, Objectives, Strategies, Mission, Outcomes
   b) Difference between objectives and outcomes
   c) Writing good learning outcomes
   d) Challenges
      i) Stakeholders without firm grasp on desired results
   ii) Etc.
3) Needs Assessments
4) Meeting Skills beyond Listening for Participants
   a) Reflecting
   b) Action Planning
   c) Networking
      i) Maximising Social Capital
   d) Improvising
   e) Collaborating
   f) Innovating
   g) Teambuilding
5) How Meeting Logistics Affect Learning
   a) Food & Beverage
   b) Breaks
   c) Room Sets
   d) Room
      i) Natural light/lighting
      ii) Color
      iii) Comfort
      iv) Temperature
6) How Agenda Items Affect Learning
   a) Theory and Guidelines
      i) Flow & Timing
      ii) Energy
      iii) Pareto's Principle
   b) Lecture/PowerPoint
   c) Entertainment
   d) Interactive Formats
   e) Etc. Other meeting elements
7) Environment (Coleman Finkel 8 types of meeting environments)
   a) Physical Environment
   b) Psychological Environment - the overall feeling in the room
   c) Influencing the Environment
      i) Physical format affects tone, communication, mood
      ii) Formats - the agenda and the way it is constructed
      iii) Emotional state of participants – a person's physical and emotional well-being are closely linked to their ability to think and to learn effectively
   d) Factors/Tools
      i) Travel stress to/from meeting
      ii) Humour
      iii) Relaxation/Recreation
      iv) Teambuilding
      v) Multisensory environments
8) Group Process
   a) Brainstorming
   b) Groupthink
   c) Decision Making Models
      i) Decision Trees
      ii) SWOT Analysis
      iii) Critical Path Analysis
      iv) Attribute Listing

v) Storyboards
vi) Unconscious Dwelling
vii) Etc.

d) Mind Mapping
e) Facilitation
f) Graphic Facilitation
g) Voting
    i) Electronic Surveys
    ii) Index Card Polling
    iii) Dots
    iv) Multi-voting
h) Social Networking Tools

9) Formats to Liven up Meetings
    a) Structured Introductions
    b) Best Practices Exchange
    c) Poster Learning
    d) Learning Lounge
    e) Charitable teambuilding
    f) Panel Discussion
    g) Debates
    h) Break-out Sessions
        i) Case Studies
    j) Structured Questions Roundtable
    k) Colloquium
    l) Hands-on Demonstrations
    m) Workshop
    n) Buzz Groups
    o) World Café format
    p) Open Space Technology (Harrison Owen)
    q) Peer-to-Peer Learning
    r) Appreciate Inquiry

10) Visual Aids
    a) Advantages to using visual aids
    b) Criteria for good visual aids
    c) Examples
        i) Computer slide presentation
        ii) Handouts
        iii) Flipchart
        iv) Slides
        v) Film/video clips
        vi) Video and audio presentations
        vii) Book marks or wallet cards
        viii) Charts
        ix) Demonstrations
        x) Displays/exhibits
        xi) Graphs
        xii) Maps
        xiii) Newsletters
        xiv) Objects or models
        xv) Photographs
        xvi) Posters
        xvii) Sketches
        xviii) Storyboards
        xix) Tip sheets
        xx) Word charts
        xxi) Whiteboards
        xxii) Workbooks
        xxiii) Combinations such as a word chart with a sketch or map
    d) Designing better visual aids
        i) Handouts
        ii) Others

11) Meeting Roles
    a) Review of roles
    b) Use of outside facilitators
    c) Models
        i) Six Hat Thinking (Edward De Bono)
        ii) Etc.

12) Coaching Speakers for Success
    a) Speaker Prep
    b) Speaker Guidelines

13) Fostering Creativity and Innovation

14) Extending the Meeting
    a) Daily conference reports
    b) Newsletters
    c) Report
    d) On site summary reports
    e) Translation
    f) Reports following the meeting
    g) Audio Archives
    h) Learning Content Management systems

15) Ethics/Legal Issues
    a) Copyright laws

b) Intellectual Property
c) ADA (only for US meetings)

16) Technology
   a) Podcasts
   b) Wikis
   c) Blogs
   d) Audio archives

17) Evaluation
   a) Closing the loop
   b) Benefits of evaluation
      i) Determine success
      ii) Identify strengths and weaknesses
      iii) Compare meeting costs to the benefits
      iv) Decide who should participate in future meetings
      v) Identify which participants were best suited for the meeting content
      vi) Reinforce major points of the presentation
      vii) Gather data for future meetings
      viii) Determine if the meeting was the appropriate solution for the need
   c) Chain of Impact
      i) Level 0 – Statistics
      ii) Level 1 – Reaction
      iii) Level 2 – Learning
      iv) Level 3 – Application
      v) Level 4 – Business Impact
      vi) Level 5 – Return on Investment
   d) Evaluation Steps
   e) Evaluation Tools/Methods

18) The Future
   a) Technology
   b) Demand for Customized Content

The above curriculum for a Meeting Architecture degree, assembled by Sue Tinnish early in 2007, is a good start. More study elements need to be added in the scientific, the Networking and the Motivational areas.

Degrees & certification

A Master's degree is the best thing that could happen to the concept of Meeting Architecture. It will generate an army of frontline soldiers, missionaries and scouts who will guide the industry forward through new terrain.

The need for education will be much wider than a fulltime course. Many of the current senior meeting planners would be interested in part-time courses or certification. Graduating students in meeting management may prefer a summer course, other schools may add crucial elements to enrich their existing courses in meeting management. Meeting owners could benefit from a one-day course, hotel conference managers from a five-day course or one-year online education. There must be a potential of hundreds of consultants and even more senior meeting planners who would go for a Certificate in Meeting Architecture CMA. Meeting designers, marketing people, PCOs, DMCs and many others would improve their position by attaining such a certificate.

All kinds of course formats need to be created to cater for all of these different needs. Whatever the course is called and whatever format it has, a continuing education programme will be necessary. Technology evolves, new formats become available, new research is made public.

Every Master's degree and eventually PhD will also generate much-needed research for the content side of the industry. A thesis on the quantification and qualification of networking at conferences is just one such area. Every student will generate more information thus making the profession grow. And PhDs will act as resources for literature and more education in many shapes and forms.

The Students

The students who would take such courses would be very different and range from high school students to senior meeting planners. Their needs would be different too. This list offers just a few ideas but obviously, once the curriculum is established, workbooks provided and existing books selected, courses can be created for any group of students.

Institution	Format	Students	Length and method
Associations or private organisations	Certification	Senior meeting professionals (planners, PCOs, conference managers in hotels, consultants)	5 days + books + exam OR a one year evening course or an online course
Universities	Summer class	Graduates in meeting management	2 or 3 weeks
	Post-graduate course		
Universities and polytechs	Part of degree in meeting management	Starting students	Selectable as an optional package
Universities	Master's in Meeting Architecture	Graduates in meeting management, Bachelor's in marketing or communication	- A summer course - an additional year - a separate Master's - a one year evening course - an online course

Potential educational formats and their length with possible institutions to organise them and potential students for these courses.

Continuing education - staying up to date

Universities which organise a degree in Meeting Architecture will also have a lot of work in order to stay up to date. The Meeting Support Institute will gladly organise taskforces which collect the valuable novelties in science and technology so all can use the same resourses to adapt their curricula annually. Academic membership of the Meeting Support Institute is already in place and Dr Elling Hamso is one of the MSI board members who would certainly be willing to contribute. The current knowledge base of the Meeting Support Institute has 26 books, just to name one category. This could be the resource for academics to construct and update their curriculum.

The mere fact that a degree or certification in Meeting Architecture will exist is going to be an eye-opener for many meeting owners, marketing managers and the corporate C level. Today, everyone looks in different directions to find various things to help them with the content side of their meetings. There is no term for what "Meeting Architect" implies. Some meeting organisers think they can do it, some will tell their marketing department to come on board, others will work with their communication company, a production company or a designer. Because most meeting organisers have different ideas of what it is they need to make the meeting work, they all look in different directions. Once they understand there is a Meeting Architecture profession they will probably look for just such a person. And once they have worked with one, they may understand that this specialist has everything they were looking for and more. The Meeting Architect will, based on the title alone, be accepted in the analysing and designing phase. It will sound logical for a Meeting Architect to ask questions and know all about building a good meeting. This is much more difficult for an AV person, a creative director or a PCO: these are all perceived as operational. Not so with an architect: a Meeting Architect obviously must know much more about these things and so his or her advice will more acceptable...

the effect of the title

Meeting Architect

innovative presentation techniques

The job market

The proof of the pudding is in the eating – we will have to see, based on the first students, if the corporate world is open to the idea of Meeting Architecture. I guess that when they look at the budgets people spend on meetings today it makes a lot of sense for them to hire Meeting Architects. Corporate meeting or conference departments will be hiring one to start with. When successful, they may hire more to team up with the meeting planners they have. PD (professional development) managers in associations are the perfect job opening for Meeting Architects. In many cases there will be someone with association background or meeting background only and PD will benefit greatly from Meeting Architect skills and knowledge. Just as we see the CMP (Certification for Meeting Professionals) today in the US, many meeting planner vacancies are requesting a CMP candidate or list CMP as a plus for candidates. Similarly, in the coming decade or two the Master's degree or certificate in Meeting Architecture may become crucial for the relevant positions.

CONCLUSION a degree in Meeting Architecture:

The chicken and the egg: will a degree in Meeting Architecture create the profession? Or is the profession so much needed that the degree is just a matter of filling the gap?

Whatever it is, a degree or any shape or form of formal education will create the profession and therefore help the industry forward. Of the teachers and professors who have read this far, I imagine some will be able to picture a successful new post-graduate course for their school or university.

Looking at the potential curriculum, a one-year full-time course seems the minimum. Shorter, part-time and summer courses are all welcome initiatives as stepping stones in the process and valuable education for professionals.

9. Meeting Architecture and the industry

The effect of Meeting Architecture as a profession will obviously not reshape the industry in one day. It will be a slow and growing process and no-one will therefore have to make fast and radical choices. On the other hand, some of the effects as described below, start now and we can influence more if we take pro-active steps today.

The effect on organisations

Corporations

Corporations may revisit their organisational charts for planning meetings. The management assistant or meeting planner who now organises the logistics can be accompanied by a Meeting Architect for the content side – a duo to support the meeting owner.
The meeting planner can do a better job with a certificate in Meeting Architecture for small and medium sized meetings. For larger and more complicated meetings the meeting planner can team up with a Meeting Architect.

Larger conference departments could create a section for Meeting Architecture and become a one-stop shop for meeting owners, doing both logistics and the meeting content.

Procurement can develop a separate strategy (SOP) for meeting content, for different suppliers with different procurement approaches taking into account creativity which can not be commoditised.

The board of a large corporation, or its CEO, CFO, CMO, VP Marketing, VP education, etc., could approve a methodology (SOP) for managing the content at big spending meetings.

Associations

As real meetings and conferences are high on the association's list of member benefits, improving them is key to an association's existence. Improving the core reason of existence for conferences through professional Meeting Architecture is therefore of strategic importance.

Many tools provide branding opportunities that will enable associations to attract more and new sponsor revenue.

Large associations may decide to hire a Meeting Architect for a job opening for a PD (Professional Development) manager.

Certification or other education in Meeting Architecture for current PD staff will be welcomed by all.

Agencies

PCOs, event agencies and independent meeting planners will all increase their value to clients when applying Meeting Architecture in their work.
Larger marketing agencies may decide to start a specialised Meeting (and event) Architecture department.
New Meeting Architecture agencies or free-lancers will appear and could be hired by agencies.

Depending on the amount of meeting work, any agency may choose for diversification or specialisation. The split of event/meeting departments into logistics and content departments makes a lot of sense and hiring of staff can be carried out with these two specialisations in mind.

The production companies

A production company which hires a Meeting Architect will widen its service package. They will create the educational experience, the networking moments or systems and motivational activities on the content side of meetings in an array much wider than the big stage production alone. Their influence will increase and their added value will grow.

Current event producers are also candidates to become Meeting Architects.

Companies with meeting support tools

Companies with meeting support tools such as networking technology, will be part of the curriculum for Meeting Architecture. How their products or services work is something which will be taught and demonstrated to students. These companies will have great advocates in graduate Meeting Architects. The Meeting Architect will be able to explain the use of tools and services for supporting certain objectives of their client, the meeting owner. The Meeting Architect will understand the possibilities of such a complex product and be able to match them to his client's objectives.

The effect on individuals

Meeting owners

For meeting owners, working with a Meeting Architect will be like a dream come true. The meeting owner today has very few people to go to for help for analysing and designing meetings. The help they get from their marketing department or agency is limited. In a Meeting Architect they will find a guide and soul mate. The Meeting Architect asks the right questions and has all the answers to challenges which were never even addressed. The meeting owner will be much more successful in creating an appropriate programme and in deploying the right systems and tools to make the effect of the meeting stronger and more lasting.

Meeting planners

Meeting planners will have the choice of specialising. If a seasoned meeting planner wishes to become a Meeting Architect, that is an option. If a meeting planner loves the hospitality side of the work, that is also an option. Having a Meeting Architect to focus on the content side enables the planner to specialise in her or his area. The meeting planner can focus fully on all the challenges and new developments in meeting planning without also having to cope with the content side of meetings.

The effect on industries

Tourism industry

One of the major opportunities we have is the meetings connection with the tourism industry. The historic connection on the logistics side with venues and destinations makes a lot of sense and, moving on from there, cultivating and nurturing Meeting Architecture also makes a lot of sense. Some people will argue that there is not a lot of connection between tourism and meeting content, but I would argue it is 'the best place to call home' since it is the only place where the meetings industry resides.

'the best place to call home'

As meetings and conferences for many players in the tourism industry are a crucial part of their revenue, the industry has a stake in improving meetings and thus securing the meetings industry. Meeting Architecture will do just that by professionalising the content side of meetings. Having Meeting Architects in organisations in addition to the current meeting planners will serve as a lifeline when the economy retreats. Rather than cutting budgets, corporations with Meeting Architects may invest when they understand the value of meetings more clearly.

Travel industry

More than 13% of airline revenue in the US comes from meetings, meaning that the travel industry too has a stake in improving and securing meetings. Unstable turnover influenced by economic and security issues can be stabilised by strategically anchoring meetings; a similar stake to that of the tourism and hospitality industry.

ultimately the meetings industry and its stakeholders can only benefit

Hospitality industry

$36.8 bilion is 32.4% of the total US hotel revenue generated by the meetings industry. This can grow only if meetings become more professional and more strategically anchored. Fluctuations caused by economic and security matters may be flattened out when meetings demonstrate ROI and their ability to increase ROI.

The hotel chains of this world are among the largest entities in the industry. Their decision to co-create this profession as a lifeline for the future will be crucial to the speed of success.

Hotels can not only support this movement, they can be part of it. The story about Lotte Marie Roesgaard (p. 50) from Comwell Denmark shows one example of how hotels or venues in general can benefit from a new focus on the content side.

The meeting industry associations

Associations for meeting planners and other industry associations will attract new types of members. Diversity will grow and the gender balance may return. The educational offerings at association conferences will increase in number and diversity and the knowledge base will increase. Networking at conferences will become more varied.

Associations of meeting planners and their suppliers may consider a future programme to attract new players such as Meeting Architects and meeting support companies. At first these will be less easy to convince and retain, and supporting their membership may be necessary. Associations may also decide to focus on the hospitality side and leave the meeting content side to others.

An example of the industry moving towards meeting content:

"How Adults Learn, Now" in PCMA's Convene

Convene, the official magazine of the Professional Convention Management Association (PCMA), is publishing a series of articles titled, "How Adults Learn, Now." This series of about 10 articles is written by Glen C. Ramsborg, PhD and Sue Tinnish. The series is published from 2008 onwards and it will be very useful for those that are interested in the educational side of their meetings.
This Convene series, "How Adults Learn, Now," is intended to offer meeting professionals a new paradigm, focused on optimizing the adult learning experience. This first article describes how four major factors - learning environments, fragmented audiences, technology, and networks - all impact how adults learn.
If you want to read more, you can visit the magazine on line (www.pcma.org) or subscribe to Convene on http://www.pcma.org/Convene/Subscribe.htm

The meeting industry trade shows

It is clear that Meeting Architects will be looking for a different set of suppliers than today's meeting planners. Trade shows are already moving in the right direction. IMEX has the meeting support area and EIBTM the MPI Technology and the event services areas.

Trade shows have seen technology companies with software and online products in the logistics arena re-appear over a number of years now. The online booking, registration, event or conference management softwares are products of interest to current visitors. It is more challenging to get the meeting content oriented companies to come and to keep them coming. Some are technology companies, but many more have non-technological products and services in the Learning, Networking and Motivational areas. Interest from meeting planners is currently limited (as demonstrated in the case on p. 42) so growing that group will take a sustained effort. More and more diverse offerings on the trade-show floor will clearly improve the service of these shows to the industry. It may, however, take a few years and the strong support of the shows to enable these meeting support companies and the interest of the audience to grow into real potential.
Starting a new trade show in a few years could also be an option.

The media

The media in the meetings industry today are 95% venue and destination oriented in both editorial content and advertising. This can only become more diverse. As companies with meeting support services and products grow, so too will their marketing budgets. New advertisers will appear and new editorial topics will appear with them.

> A perfect example is what Katherine Simmons is doing at M&IT (MeetingsS & Incentive Travel) a magazine from the UK. They currently have an ongoing series of articles entitled "Anatomy of a meeting" and Katherine does some interesting market research for each one. The support of industry leaders such as M&IT's Managing Editor Martin Lewis will be instrumental.

The media can choose to mix both or, over time, decide to start a separate magazine. Once sufficient advertising can be gathered to support a magazine, someone will decide to create a specialised publication.

HeadQuarters magazine with the Meeting Support Institute has made a step in that direction with a first ever (annual) Meetings Technology supplement in March 2008. With 24 pages and about 10 pages of advertising, this seems a way forward and we hope other magazines will follow.

Meeting management education

The potential effect here is obvious. Universities and other educational institutes have the opportunity to create a new degree alongside their meeting management or event management degrees. Meeting Architecture material can be added to the current curriculum for meeting management. A more ambitious programme would be an additional specialist year in Meeting Architecture after a course in meeting management. For educational institutions, it will result in a more complete curriculum and better armed graduates. The range of professions a student can choose from becomes more complete and therefore the courses become more attractive.

10. Conclusions

The meeting industry is mature in organising the shell: logistics and hospitality. It is now ready to develop the substance: the content and objectives side of meetings.

Content is about objectives: the Learning objectives, the Networking objectives and the Motivational objectives. Identifying those objectives needs a standardised and structured approach.

Meeting Support is what you can do to improve results for those objectives. Companies in meeting support are small and dispersed and need to be invited into the industry.

The tools for Meeting Support are CHATTY: Conceptual, Human, Art, Technical, TechnologY and there are more than 1,000 tools most of which are unknown to the industry.

A lot of scientific research data and knowledge exists but is spread across many different disciplines (psychology, sociology, musicology, anthropology, biology, neurology...). Many industries also contain knowledge in many different fields: Training, marketing, education, corporate communications... We need to invite players from these industries to help us build an extensive knowledge base. This needs to be assembled and translated for meetings in order to create textbooks.

There are no trade shows, magazines, courses or organisations focusing on the content side of meetings.
There are no degrees or formal education focusing on the content side of meetings. The complexity is vast so a degree in Meeting Architecture will be appropriate.

IDEA: A Meeting Architect Identifies a meeting's objectives, Designs the content side of the meeting based on those objectives, helps with Execution and Assesses the results of the meeting. The holistic approach will result in a better spend and improved ROI.

For all players in the meeting industry, both buyers and suppliers, the creation of a degree in Meeting Architecture will present, opportunity, career options, growth, improvement, more influence and strategic positioning.

Only if the hospitality industry embraces, helps to organise and fully supports the development of the profession of Meeting Architect will the creation of Meeting Architecture be possible.

With Meeting Architecture included, the industry will rightfully call itself the meeting industry and become of higher and global strategic importance.

Contact the author with remarks and suggestions at
maarten.vanneste@abbit.eu

11. Bibliography

The Economic Impact of Meetings, Conventions, Exhibitions, and Incentive Travel.
McLean, VA: Convention Industry Council. (CIC. 2005).

Open SpaceTechnology.
Harrison, O. (Berrett-Koehler, 1997)

Training with a beat: the teaching power of music
(Lenn Millbower, Stylus, Sterling, 2000)

Objectives to outcomes: your contract with the learner
(Glen C. Ramsborg, PCMA, Alabama, 1995)

Learning Meetings and Conferences in Practice
(Steen Elsborg, Ib Ravn, People's Press, Denmark, 2007)

Wisdom of Crowds.
(James Surowiecky, Little-Brown, Great Britain, 2004)

The Big Book of presentation games
(Scannell and Newstrom, McGraw-Hill, New York, 1997)

The Big Book of team building games
(Newstrom and Scannell, McGraw-Hill, New York, 1998)

The Big Book of meeting games
(Caroselli, McGraw-Hill, New York, 2002)

The IAF handbook of group facilitation
(Sandy Schuman (IAF), Jossey-Bass, San Francisco, 2005)

Proving The Value of Meetings & Events
(Jack Phillips, Ph.D., Monica Myhill and James B. McDonough, 2006)

Transferring Learning to Behavior
(Donald L. Kirkpatrick and James D. Kirkpatrick, Ph.D., Berrett-Koehler,
San Francisco, 2005)

Books to be written

Meeting Content Analysis
A Methodology / SOP for the big spend meetings.

Meeting Design:
A comprehensive overview of all formats and tools to design meetings based on objectives.

Meeting Architecture II:
The Curiculum: A comprehensive overview of what a Meeting Architect should know.

Meeting Support for Learning at Meetings:
What meeting organisers can do and should know to improve the learning by participants at their meetings.

Meeting Support for Networking at Meetings:
What meeting organisers can do and should know to improve the networking among participants at their meetings.

Meeting Support for Motivation at Meetings:
What meeting organisers can do and should know to improve the motivation of participants at their meetings.

The Great Book of Meeting Support:
What meeting planners can do to improve the learning, networking and motivation in the participant population.

The Great Book of Meeting Support Tools:
A comprehensive overview of concepts, human input, art and creative tools, technical tools and technology.

Psychology in Meetings:
An overview of applicable psychology for learning, networking and motivation in meetings and conferences.

Neurology and Biology for Meetings:
An overview of neurological and biological knowledge with an impact on the Learning, Networking and Motivation of participants at meetings.

Hybrid Meetings:
Where virtual meetings meet real meetings

Sociology for Meetings and Conferences

Music, Drama and other arts for Meetings

ETC.

Thank you note

There are too many individuals I need to thank for their help and support. First of all my father for his early vision and my mother for all the support she gave to get an 18 year old going. Dirk Reyn for helping me see the potential of meetings and conferences and all our clients for trusting us with innovation.
The Abbit Team that allowed me to take the time to write this book. My wife Kristin for putting up with me during the process. MPI for its great community. Carole McKellar and the CMM team for helping me with the Meeting Support Institute business plan. Elling Hamso and Damien Hutt for putting me on the right track. Rob Davidson and Martin Lewis for being such big supporters.
And then there are the many people who helped me with the content of this book, reviewing it and commenting in many helpful ways. Among the major contributors were: Sue Tinnish, Glen Ramsborg, Richard John, Tony Carey, Mary Boone and Ed Bernacki. And also, Joyce and Miranda, Carina and Dale, Ib, Lars and Lotte, Janet, Dorcy, Els and Kristel, Sam, Naunton, Paula and Ray, Robin, Ester, Gregg and Teun, Anna and Katherine.
And finally Martin O'Connor for improving language and spelling, Sonia Trouvé for making it look good and Stephan Beyens for managing the whole printing process until just in time delivery.

Without you and many others, these words would make no sense.

Maarten

Addendum to the 3rd Print

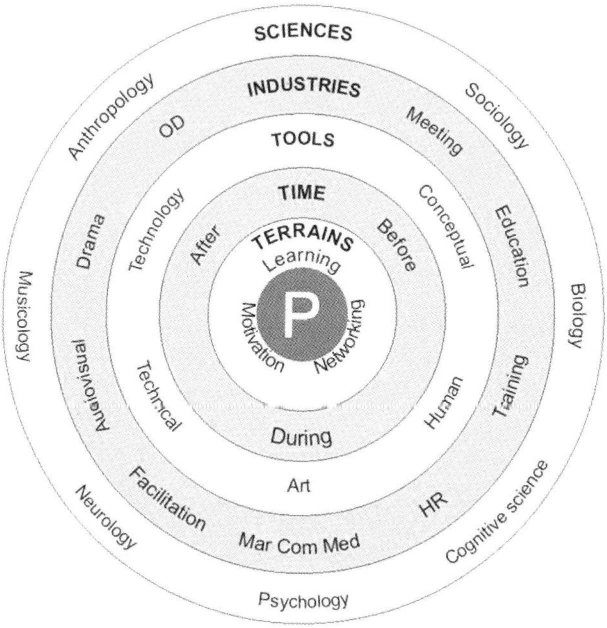

The Meeting Architecture knowledge graph

(AKA the red core onion graph)

This graph was developed after the first print as part of the Meeting Architecture Process or MAP™. MAP is the Standard Operating Procedure for developing the content side of meetings and events. See www.meetingarchitecture.com.

The P in the centre:
In Meeting Architecture we focus on participant action: what the participant will do (differently) after the meeting and based on the meeting.

1. First ring around the P: We focus on three groups of objectives (see Page 56): Learning, Networking and Motivation. We also call these terrains because they are distinctive areas of focus and activity. These are all level two objectives (see ROI on Page 45).

2. Second ring: We look at 'when' we can do something to support the objectives (see Page 84): before, during and after the meeting.

3. Third Ring: 'What' can we do? To ensure we look at all possible 'tools' (see Page 82) we have the CHATTY acronym for: Conceptual tools, Human tools, Art tools, Technical tools, and TechnologY tools.

4. Fourth Ring: In order to select and deploy the right tools, we need to know and understand the applicable techniques and methods available from sister industries (Page 120).

5. Fifth ring: To maximise the potential effect of a tool or a combination of tools, we need to understand the relevant knowledge from ancillary sciences (Page 118).

Going inwards towards the P, we can look at several examples:

• Use psychology and techniques from HR to select the right tool that you can use after the meeting to maintain the connections with new contacts for the participant.
• Use cognitive science and techniques from organisational development (OD) to achieve the right concept during the presentation in order to optimise knowledge about the new product in the participant's mind.

For the latest on Meeting Architecture:
www.meetingarchitecture.org The official website for the Meeting Architecture Project
www.meetingarchitecture.com The author's website
Facebook Group 'Meeting Architecture': the on-line community